THE ADLARD CC
BALTIC CRUISING

THE ADLARD COLES BOOK OF
BALTIC CRUISING

ADLARD
COLES

LONDON · OXFORD · NEW YORK · NEW DELHI · SYDNEY

ADLARD COLES
Bloomsbury Publishing Plc
50 Bedford Square, London, WC1B 3DP, UK
29 Earlsfort Terrace, Dublin 2, Ireland

BLOOMSBURY, ADLARD COLES and the
Adlard Coles logo are trademarks of
Bloomsbury Publishing Plc

First published in Germany as *Sehnsuchtsrevier Ostsee* by Delius Klasing & Co KG 2019
First published in Great Britain 2023

A catalogue record for this book is available from the British Library

Library of Congress Cataloguing-in-Publication data has been applied for

ISBN: PB: 978-1-3994-0126-5;
ePub: 978-1-3994-0125-8;
ePDF: 978-1-3994-0124-1

2 4 6 8 10 9 7 5 3 1

Typeset in 10/13pt Optima by Carr Design Studio
Printed and bound in India by Replika Press

To find out more about our authors and books visit www.bloomsbury.com and sign up for our newsletters

CONTENTS

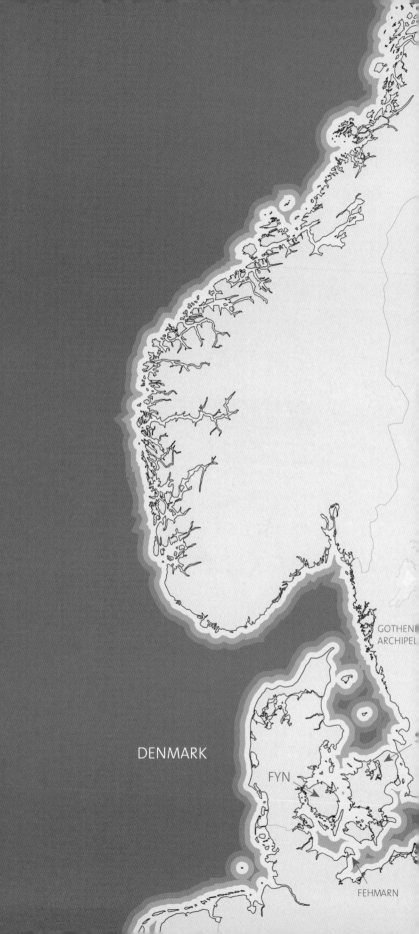

DENMARK

GOTHEN
ARCHIPEL

FYN

FEHMARN

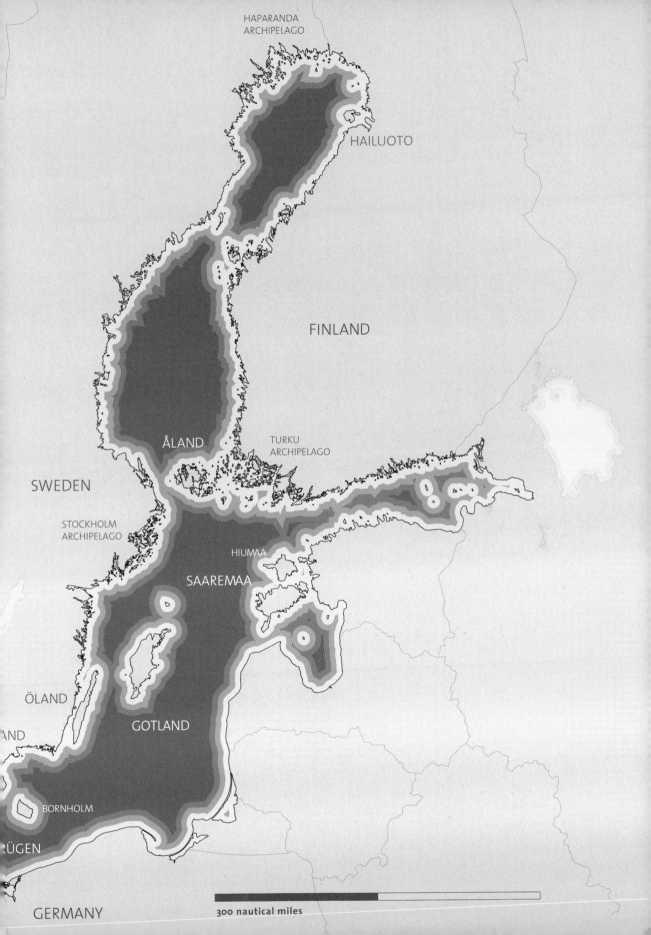

HAPARANDA
ARCHIPELAGO

HAILUOTO

FINLAND

ÅLAND

TURKU
ARCHIPELAGO

SWEDEN

STOCKHOLM
ARCHIPELAGO

HIUMAA

SAAREMAA

ÖLAND

GOTLAND

BORNHOLM

RÜGEN

GERMANY

300 nautical miles

1 FLENSBURG FJORD

Fahrradfahren und Angeln auf den Brücken nicht gestattet
Der Eigentümer

Betreten der Hafenanlagen auf eigene Gefahr
Eltern haften für ihre Kinder
Der Eigentümer

Hunde anleinen!

The 250-metre-long wooden jetty of Wackerballig Marina in the south of Geltinger Bay.

Between two worlds: paradise and hustle and bustle lie close together in the German-Danish border region.

1 THE BEACONS

The fairways of the Flensburg Fjord are continuously marked with directional and leading lights. When approaching from the sea at night, the following lights with their coloured segments are particularly important: Gammel Pøl in the south-east of Als (Oc (3) WRG. 15s, 20m, 11/8M), Kegnæs at the eastern end of the Kegnæs peninsula (Oc. WRG. 5s, 32m, 12/9M) and Kalkgrund on its sea position north of the Kalkgrund reef (Iso. WRG. 8s, 22m, 14-12M, Horn Mo(FS) 30s), plus further on the tower on the Holnis peninsula (Iso. WRG. 6s, 32m, 13-10M). The lighthouse of Falshöft is only a landmark; its light is extinguished.

In high season, quays at Danish city harbours are often busy, such as here at Sønder Havnegade in the southern harbour of Sønderborg.

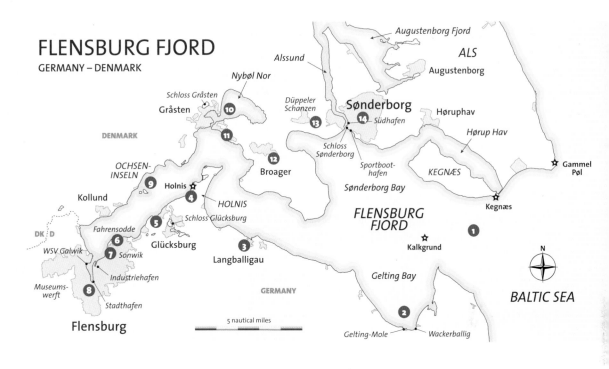

FLENSBURG FJORD
GERMANY – DENMARK

A peaceful view over Sønderborg's marina. The Kegnæs peninsula can be seen in the top right.

There are lots of places to moor to jetties and buoys on the Baltic coast, as here in Gelting-Mole. Free moorings are usually recognisable by a green sign.

2 BAY OF GELTINGEN

In the south of the bay there are two well-protected marinas: Wackerballig, whose jetty is 250 metres off the coast and can only be reached via a wooden bridge from the beach, and Gelting-Mole, which is located directly on the shore, but as a certified four-star marina offers many services.

3 LANGBALLIGAU

The district harbour of Langballigau, which is also home to a number of fishermen, is very cosy and green, with a café-restaurant and close to the beach. If you are lucky, you can even get your fresh catch directly from the boat.

4 SCHAUSENDE

North of the Holnis peninsula, even recreational boats must keep to the buoyed fairway: west of light post '6', the water depth is less than 1 metre. Until a few years ago, there was a light buoy at this spot, which was called the 'mother-in-law' – anyone who crossed it was run aground. On the west side of the peninsula is the Schausende Marina, where Club Nautic welcomes visiting sailors.

A 1:3.5-scale replica of the 18th-century West Indies brig *Foreenigen* at the Flensburg museum shipyard.

Green idyll: many of the fjord ports are found in the middle of nature, with the beach right around the corner. Some ports are more natural and others are more cultivated, like in Langballigau.

5 GLÜCKSBURG

The spacious and beautifully situated yacht harbour is the base of the Flensburg Sailing Club and the Hanseatic Yacht School and offers full services. It is also the best starting point for an excursion to the moated castle of Glücksburg, which, with its four striking corner towers, is one of the most significant and magnificent buildings of the Renaissance in Northern Europe. Guided tours take place daily at 2pm in July and August, though check in advance whether you need to book. The grounds include the castle park and rose garden.

6 FAHRENSODDE

The large marina of the Flensburg Yacht Club and the Flensburg Sailing Association is in a quiet location. Both Glücksburg (7 kilometres away) and Flensburg (6 kilometres) are still within easy reach from here by bicycle.

7 SONWIK

A complete residential quarter for the high-end market has been created on former naval grounds next to the marina – including a harbour promenade. The atmosphere is much more urban here, and the 3 kilometres to the centre of Flensburg can be comfortably covered in ten minutes by bus on line 5. The marina's range of services is second to none.

8 FLENSBURG

There are a number of harbours in Flensburg that offer visitor berths, but the most central location is in the city harbour, run by the company 'im jaich' on the east bank.

There are guest moorings in several places in Flensburg, including the city harbour and Galwik water sports club on the west bank.

The letters GGGMF can be found above the gate at Glücksburg Palace, a motto that can be translated to 'God grant happiness with peace'.

The massive twin spires of the church in Broager, Denmark, can be seem from the fjord and make a good landmark for navigation.

In the cosy restaurant Heimathafen Flensburg right by the jetty, you can enjoy 'southern German cuisine with the best local produce' – the colourful menu ranges from crab soup to cheese spaetzle (dumplings). However, it is only a few minutes' walk to the city centre with its numerous other restaurants. Afterwards, the shore excursion might take you to the maritime museum and the museum shipyard, where you can experience old boatbuilding craftsmanship live.

9 THE OX ISLANDS

Store Okseø and its even smaller, uninhabited neighbour are the only islands in the Flensburg Fjord. Nevertheless, there is a ferry pier, a nice restaurant and about 30 places for visiting sailors on the floating and mooring pontoons.

10 NYBØL NOR

Under the bascule bridge from Egernsund you can pass from Rinkenæs Bay to Nybøl Nor, an idyllic inland lake connected to the fjord. Moorings are available at Marina Fiskenæs in Gråsten. Gråsten Slot, about a kilometre to the north, is the summer residence of the Danish queen.

11 MARINA MINDE

This well-equipped marina with a beach and holiday complex is located on the Danish side opposite the Holnis peninsula. It's a good starting point for a trip to Broager, 4 kilometres away.

Marina Minde offers guest berths just over 4km from Broager, though a lot of skippers also have permanent berths here.

View of one of the jetties of the Flensburg city marina. The slender brick tower that rises in the background is St Jürgen's Church.

Dybbøl mill was rebuilt after being destroyed during the war of 1864. Monuments to the fallen of both sides can be found throughout the area.

Gelting-Mole marina is one of the larger harbours on the Flensburg Fjord.

A relaxed atmosphere during summer at Flensburg's museum harbour.

decisive battle in the Second Schleswig War between Denmark and Prussia took place at Dybbøl, ending in the defeat of the Danes. An exhibition commemorates the bloody events of those days, and a walk across the ridge with a sweeping view over the fjord will give you pause for thought.

14 SØNDERBORG

Located at the southern exit of the Alssund, Sønderborg is a must on every fjord cruise: visitors have the choice between the wall in Sydhavnen between the bascule bridge and the castle (quickly occupied in summer) and the marina a little outside. With several supermarkets, the shopping facilities are good, and those who don't mind the higher prices can also try one of the many restaurants. There are some good ones right by the harbour. The castle houses the Regional Museum of Southern Jutland, and the Battle of Dybbøl site on the eastern shore is just under 4 kilometres away.

Text: Christian Tiedt

12 BROAGER

This is the only village in Denmark with a double-spired church. The interior is decorated with frescoes, the oldest motifs of which date back to around the year 1200.

13 DYBBØL

This small town marks a dark chapter in the history of Germany and Denmark. In 1864, the

Even in the high season it's
still possible to find quiet,
secluded anchorages like
this one off Sejerø.

2 THE KATTEGAT

One man who knows the Kattegat like no other is Niels Skouby. If you follow his suggestions, you will find the most secluded and unspoilt places in the area.

In the high season, the strait sometimes resembles a fairground. This is often unpleasant, but fortunately there are alternatives. With his markings on the nautical chart, an expert guides you to the magical places nearby – and yet far away from the hustle and bustle.

They are still just squiggles on the sea chart, pencilled circles around a few yellow spots and lines on the paper. Niels Skouby is bent over his table in the cockpit, tanned, wearing a sleeveless T-shirt and an amber point around his neck, his teeth shining in the sun like white bathroom tiles. 'Head here,' he says. 'And you should look at this, too.' He draws two more squiggles on the map. 'Good for anchoring, and virtually no one around.'

Skouby is already over 70. The Dane has been sailing around the region since he first sat in a dinghy on the Limfjord at the age of four. He has spent his life touring the strait and neighbouring waters on yachts. A better

The beautiful beach of Æbelø could inspire the inner artist in many sailors.

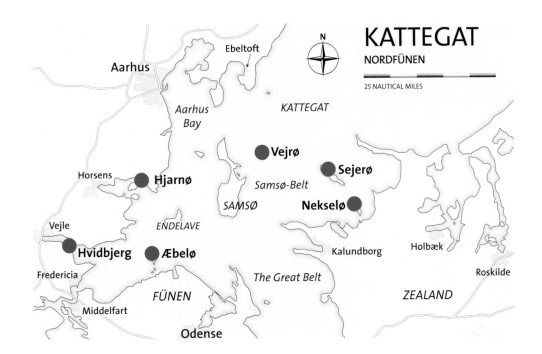

guide would be hard to find. So, when asked about the quiet islands and peaceful bays in the area, about secluded and unspoilt places where hardly any yachts ever stray, he draws his squiggles on the map without hesitation. Normally, this question cannot be answered in the widely navigated Danish island kingdom. Especially not during the high season, when the harbours on Samsø, Tunø or Anholt, for example, are so crowded that it is sometimes almost unbearable. Niels Skouby says goodbye, he has to move on, at the moment his sailing schedule is strictly timed. He is sailing three folk musicians from island to island to their gigs.

The old sailor has left a sea chart with six circles and a few short notes in the margin: 'Only go when there is a southerly wind', 'Only goats live there', 'Private island, but you may moor at the small jetty', 'Nice people there, please give them my regards.'

On board, the tension grows because it is actually impossible to find what we are looking for – as if we wanted to look at a wonderful piazza in Venice that no tourist has yet discovered. And our doubts are not lessened by the fact that the perfect sailing weather has already caused a lot of traffic on the water on the journey through the Danish South Sea.

In Marstal, the yachts were packed into the harbour, and on Skarø, Strynø and the like, the boats were bobbing fender to fender, so that sometimes you could hardly see the water for all the vessels. On the way, there was also a lot of activity. In the bay of Lyø, the yachts almost sailed over each other to find a free spot to anchor during the afternoon rally. Middelfart, the last port before the strait, had been full to capacity.

After a short journey from there to the north-east, a light brown ridge appeared in the sea, the first squiggle on the nautical chart: the mostly uninhabited island of Æbelø, with a pale sand beach and a narrow headland. To the north, a neat cliff, behind it forest and

Æbelø lies just beyond the Little Belt. The island is inhabited only by deer and hares.

the tip of the lighthouse. A good ten yachts are anchored in the western bay; with shifting winds, they could move to the eastern side in an instant. Æbelø is a kind of double bay, divided by a thin strip of earth that disappears into the water to the south. The dinghy is quickly put to water.

On the beach, on sand that is still warm in the evening, there is evidence of animals. Deer inhabit the small, narrow Æbelø, eat up the island's grass and gradually become a plague. A biologist and his students are currently in the field station at the lighthouse to check the population. The biologist says: 'We have counted over 500 deer, above 250 they can be culled, otherwise the vegetation of the island suffers.' And indeed, the deer are migrating from Funen, wading and swimming

across the headland to the island when the water level is low.

An absolute silence lies over the small islet. There is only one farm in the seclusion, run by the nature conservationist Aage V. Jensens. But usually no one is there at this time of year; the building is important for feeding the deer in winter. The foundation also wants to protect a pair of lovers: two rare white-tailed eagles. Visitors, it warns on the signs, should not disturb them while they are breeding.

Only on the eastern shore is there any sign of human presence: a fishing boat that has sunk up to its neck lies in the shallow water, its floorboards and planks already spread over a wide area on the shore by the winter storms, where they are slowly rotting away. Panels and locker doors lie around, overgrown with barnacles, encrusted with sand and silt.

Beautiful, quiet Æbelø – a speck of wooded and grassy earth in the sea. On the shore in the evening, a sailor sits in the sand, drawing. He has his paints and brushes with him and records the mood on paper. A watercolour of clouds, sky, sea and peace – and not the slightest hint of the large throng of yachts.

Where to next? A look at the sea chart. Niels Skouby has distributed his squiggles neatly between the Little Belt and the Great Belt, between Jutland and Zealand, all of them north of Funen. One of them marks Hjarnø, a tiny island in the Horsens Fjord. When we stop at Endelave, we encounter the large caravan of yachts on their way to or from the Belts. It is so crowded that the harbourmaster instructs the skippers to stuff the hulls of their yachts between the boats moored in the berths. Long queues have formed at the mini-golf course, thick smoke billows into the sky from all the barbecue areas. As beautiful as Endelave is, it is not pleasant, so we quickly move on, heading north-west, in the direction of a supposed dead end at Horsens Fjord. There, like a plate of lettuce in the sea, the small island of Hjarnø soon appears.

It lies just off Snaptun and is inhabited – about a hundred souls live here – yet right now it broods as if abandoned in the heat. Not a single visiting yacht floats in the tiny harbour, and only one sailing ship is moored at the two anchor buoys in the lagoon. Instead, fishing boats float in the shallow water; over on the other side, the Danes run fish and shellfish

Only about 100 people live on Hjarnø, and sometimes even in summer it can feel deserted – even at this café.

The church on Hjarnø (the second smallest Danish church) has a reminder of the island's Viking history.

farms. Walking across the island, you also pass through a strange summer silence.

Bright fields stretch out in the east, light-green flax in the west, and a white-blue sky shines above them. The stall with the old beer advertisement is still closed, the sunshades are folded. The visitors, including the yachts, can be counted on one hand. Today there is… one. A miracle for such a picturesque spot.

As expected, there are no sanitary facilities, supermarkets or restaurants here. But there are other things to discover: Hjarnø has the second smallest church in the Danish archipelago, just up the inconspicuous country lane on the right. White stone, a few simple wooden

benches, a pulpit painted in bright green, and no one there. The door to the church is open, a warm wind blows through the old walls.

The big eye-catcher is a model of a Viking boat hanging as a votive ship in the middle of the church – the only one of its kind on the Danish islands. And it tells its story. Wedges, bones and tools from reindeer hunters have been found on the 320-hectare moraine island, dating back to 9500 BC. Later, the Vikings came here because they could easily set sail from Horsens Fjord. The church and its votive ship are reminders of these ancient Norsemen. Even today, there are ten ship-shaped stones on Hjarnø, found during excavations in 1935: the graves of the former swashbucklers at sea.

Most of Hjarnø's inhabitants are farmers, but they all seem to have flown the coop at present. The small gallery around the corner, right next to a mile-wide wheat field, seems all the more bizarre. A white house with a sandy floor, on the walls hang modern art, watercolours, abstracts in oils – and by no means kitsch. But here too: not a soul.

Where have they gone, the islanders? Out into the world for the summer holidays? To Paris, New York? In any case, there is nothing but peace and quiet on the island's vineyard, Hjarnø Vinlaug. Here they have grown over 900 vines on 0.5 hectares and press their own red and white wine, sold in bottles with attractive labels. But today there is only an abandoned rocking chair in the meadow. It serves as a symbol for the most beautiful export of the hour: the sound of silence – in the middle of the peak sailing season. You quickly get used to the sense of isolation, cruising around in a barely frequented sea area. No hunt for a berth, no neighbours on the jetty, no crew noise. It's as if you're on the

Hvidbjerg is a great place to anchor, with a breathtaking view over the Strait from the top of the dune.

move during closing hours in the Danish island paradise. An almost spiritual state, that's what it feels like.

And its value becomes even clearer in contrast to the norm. In Ballen, the best-known destination on Samsø, the place seems to be under siege. Yachts lie squeezed into packs of ten. Jet skis and stand-up paddleboarders bob between the boats; beer cans are passed from deck to deck. Early in the afternoon, the first party cruisers fill the harbour with booming music. Let's get out of here, no one really needs that. It's better to find out which lost post in the Baltic island kingdom is hidden behind Niels Skouby's next squiggle.

The boat navigates west past Kyholm, north of Lindholm. The shallow islands and lagoons up here in the sea, which mostly only kayakers can reach, glitter almost like the Maldives. But then, a little to the north, a brown ridge comes into view and a promontory jutting far into the sea. You rub your eyes: only one yacht is anchored there, sheltered behind the southern cliff, just as Niels Skouby had noted on the map. Welcome to Vejrø.

Here, apart from this one yacht, there is only water, sky and birds. Feet tread on an uninhabited island, scorched by the sun, overgrown only by bent grass and scrawny bushes. A long shingle beach curves into the sea, and at the east end stand the ruins of an old house. Only a crumbling wall remains. Beyond that: nothing but nature – only heat and brooding silence.

Yet Niels Skouby had spoken of mouflons living here, wild sheep that look like rams. And there really is one, lying on the beach in the sun. The mouflons once lived in Sardinia and Corsica, but were introduced to Northern Europe well over a hundred years ago. On some Danish islands, of all places, they still exist today, including here on Vejrø, which has been completely abandoned by humans. But there is no trace of living specimens; they must

Wonderful little corner shops like this one on Sejerø are the only place to get provisions.

On Hjarnø signposts (such as this one pointing to the beach) are sometimes made of driftwood.

The only trace of people on Æbelø is the wreck of this cutter on the island's east coast.

be hiding in the shaggy north of the island. The animals have their peace and quiet here. Boats rarely pass by, even if they could anchor in almost Mediterranean-clear water. The bay is a real dream, an inverted mirage! Unbelievable, but true. Only a few geese on sticks are to be found elsewhere, wooden dummies lying in the grass. Presumably hunters who are allowed to come here to shoot during the season have forgotten them. Wild Vejrø. A beautiful no man's island, absolutely the right setting for a Robinson Crusoe adventure if the weather is right.

The only question that soon arises – as expectations soar – is whether there are any places where not even a single foreign yacht is present, where the world belongs to you alone.

'Absolutely no one there,' Niels Skouby had scribbled on the map alongside his next squiggle, and 'picture-perfect'. So, we set course for Sejerø. Soon the island is in front of us. There is a cosy little harbour here, where two Danish pensioners sell organic beer and homemade ice cream from a caravan, where there are junk shops next to the fishermen's stalls and an old grocer's shop has been preserved in a museum. Not exactly a lot going on here. But even the small harbour feels like too much commotion after the previous pleasures. Instead, undisturbed enjoyment is promised by sailing to the south-east, once around the shallows of Sejerø Rev. And there it soon appears: the wafer-thin end of the island – nothing but a strip of sand nestled in the Baltic Sea and seeming to melt into it.

The yacht floats anchored on bright green, safely to the east or west of the Trille, depending on the wind. The waves slapping against each other reveal where the land is disappearing under the sea, where the sandbank still stretches far south beneath the surface. Seagulls and oystercatchers circle there; three lone hikers walk barefoot, strolling across the sand as if they were walking on the sea. A heavenly scene that promptly triggers philosophising about earth and water. Anchoring here becomes an experience of rare quality. All around is nothing but light and glittering sea, and yet the boat lies protected from every little wave. Conclusion in the logbook: '360-degree view, Zealand to the east, Sejerø to the north. But from here all land is very small. Mark this spot!'

Obviously, Niels Skouby knew very well what we were looking for – namely exactly this. It's actually quite simple: don't follow the lemmings, but head for the many small bays and beaches that are marked on the sea charts.

Nekselø uses the honour system – put your payment in the collection box.

There are so many more of them in Denmark. Maybe the trick is to look for a spot by instinct and echo sounder, by the colour of the water – and not by how well known it is. You quickly end up in another world, often a wonderfully sleepy one. Nekselø is a good example of this. The small island lies like a pancake of earth deep in Nekselø Bay, north of Zealand. Only 15 Danes live on the private island, which

is listed in the Association of Danish Small Islands. A cute ferry sails to and from the mainland and brings a few day visitors, but in the evening it's idle again. A few horses graze in the meadows, otherwise only the wind blows across the fields.

Those who want to reach the mini harbour must circumnavigate a few big rocks and shallow areas after an unmarked approach.

The natural beauty of Vejrø National Park Island lies only a few nautical miles from the tourist hotspot Samsø.

There is just enough room for two or three visiting yachts; in total, there are only six or seven boats moored in the small harbour of Nekselø.

Anchor at Hvidbjerg and in the evening climb the dune for beautiful views.

Basically, it's just a jetty, consisting of a few crooked planks rammed into the bay behind the breakwater. I wonder aloud if there's such a thing as a harbourmaster here? 'I'm the harbourmaster!' says the man from the neighbouring boat, who must have picked up something from the conversation. 'But I'm on holiday. Just throw the money in the blue box in the shed.' His name is Michael Høy and he is spending the holidays on his cabin cruiser *Balu*, which he recently brought from Greifswald. A harbourmaster on holiday in his own harbour? 'Yes, sounds crazy, I know,' he says. 'But nobody comes here, here I have

my peace and quiet.' Only two families live permanently on Nekselø, the others come and go throughout the year. The farmers' sons are apprenticed as electricians, they take the ferry to the mainland every morning. Yet Zealand is not a mainland at all; little Nekselø is rather an island in front of an island among many other islands. And that explains a lot. The peaceful forest out here. The silence. Also, the still life in the shed where the fishermen's photos hang, next to rusty nails, an old paint pot and four rickety sockets.

And the blue postbox, the payment machine, on which the operating instructions

The tiny harbour at Nekselø offers infinite tranquility, without any noisy parties or even a breath of wind.

are simply written in Sharpie: 'Havnepenge' [Port Dues]. What remains after Nekselø? An intensification of peacefulness and isolation? The crowning glory of Danish deceleration, if that is even possible? Perhaps this sixth circle, which Skouby drew so casually on the map. It lies on the route back south: 'Hvidbjerg'. The white mountain. Behind a cape near Middelfart, called the Trelde Næs, hidden in a bay of Vejle Fjord, the bright spot grows as you approach and takes on contours.

It rises in front of the boat to a dune almost 30 metres high, formed of pale, fine sand: the white mountain. A giant slide. A sandy lookout, with clear views from the summit across the sea to the east. At the foot of the white mountain, an old jetty reaches into the water, but it's only suitable for bathers. No harbour, no pier. So, you must anchor. And just four yachts are actually anchored. Four! It's unbelievable.

What a place. The barbecue glows in the evening, the sand is warm, the sea a blue mirror on which the boats rest as if on glass. Isolated and quiet and undisturbed. This is Denmark at the height of summer. So empty, so wide. So incredibly beautiful.

Text: Marc Bielefeld

3 LITTLE BELT AND FUNEN

Escape from the hustle and bustle – there are still quiet havens away from the crowds in the Little Belt and South Funen, you just have to find them.

If you sail through the Little and Great Belt around Funen, you will inevitably come across places like Sønderborg, Middelfart, Marstal and so on, all popular destinations with marinas that lack nothing – but which are also packed to the rafters every year in summer. These places can be avoided. A glance at the map reveals that there are numerous other treasures around the many fjords, sounds, bays, headlands and islands.

Wooden jetties nestling in reed banks, small harbours in an isolated natural landscape and modest harbour villages that lie in the shadow of their famous neighbours. But where exactly are these gems of the region hidden, and what is there to see there?

You won't find this mooring in any handbook – Føns Vig is located in a nature reserve in the Little Belt.

The small harbour of Ristinge, and the channel leading to it, were dredged to 2.7m a few years ago.

What facilities are available, and which ships take sailors there?

On a voyage around Funen, we left the well-known harbours behind and turned instead to the stylish, rarely visited places of the region. We found spots like Løverodde, Brejning, Sottrupskov or Føns – places that really bring out the complex character of the sailing area. Some of them are oases of tranquility, nestling dreamily in secluded natural surroundings, while others are cosy and down-to-earth, as well as individual, edgy harbour and landing sites. You can find out where they are on the following pages.

1 RISTINGE

A harbour in slumber. No wonder, since Ristinge on Langeland lies a little off the beaten track, and all the guides mention an access road that is heavily silted up. So even in midsummer, there are usually still places available in the tiny harbour. But that will change. As local fisherman Asger tells us on site: 'Two years ago the channel and the harbour were dredged to 2.7 metres, even in the inner basin we now have 2.6 metres.' Five green and three red closely spaced buoys point the way through the channel, directly towards a pier that can accommodate large yachts over 15 metres on all three sides.

That makes sense: Ristinge has a long history as a cargo harbour for fruit-carrying ships. Once, it was cargo sailors who moored at the small concrete pier. Today, it is fishermen who are at home here. They process their catch in an old warehouse. Electricity, water and basic sanitary facilities are available, and

Picturesque fishermen's cabins and well-kept sanitary facilities can be found on the small island of Thurø.

the annual harbour festival takes place at the end of July. It is a charming and rustic mooring, characterised by the inhabitants of the village. There is a kiosk about 700 metres away where until 4pm you can order bread rolls for the next morning.

2 THURØ

The island of Thurø, right next to Svendborg, looks like a dog's head on the map: the mouth is a deep fjord-like indentation called Thurø Bund. In the windjammer era, hundreds of ships were berthed here, and the island's inhabitants were known throughout the world as good sailors. Today, on the northern shore of the idyllic natural harbour, there are several jetties and two boatyards, which, adapted to modern times, offer a comprehensive yacht service. The Thurø Sejlklub also has its mooring below the steep bank, and there is space for visitors on the easternmost jetty. With stern buoys and no pilings, even large and wide ships can moor.

On shore there is a handful of picturesque thatched and black-painted fishermen's huts; on the lawn in front of them, fish traps and nets dry in the sun on wooden scaffolding. It is a well-maintained and friendly harbour facility with good sanitary facilities (with automatic shower tokens). In summer there is always something going on – barbecues, picnics on the wooden tables, and children and dinghy sailors launching their boats.

3 BALLEN

At the western end of Svendborg Sound, a tranquil little marina lies secluded in the shadow of the town of the same name. A little above it, next to a few pastures and paddocks, the pretty detached houses of the mini settlement of Ballen are nestled in the landscape. The lovely green surroundings invite you to go for a walk, but the most beautiful place is the bathing area right next to the harbour pier. A green meadow for ball games, a small beach and a jetty with bathing ladders make this place a children's paradise. The harbour is private, but offers visitor berths. It has the usual service facilities, but no catering options.

TIP

An artificial reef was created half a mile south-east of the harbour when the ferry M/F Ærøsund was sunk. Two yellow anchor buoys for mooring make it easier for divers to descend. The top of the funnel is only 6 metres below the surface and therefore also interesting for experienced free divers.

The small harbour of Ballen on Svendborg Sound is like an open-air swimming poor, and great for children.

The Sottrupskov jetty at Als Sund.

4 SOTTRUPSKOV

Along the shores of the narrow Alsensundet between the Danish mainland and the island of Alsen, pastures, fields, cows, farms, forests and cliffs pass by the sailor. At the northern end of the sound lies the tiny settlement of Sottrupskov. A few thatched houses stand here next to a copse on the hillside. In front of them, a long wooden jetty juts out into the deep sound. The narrow channels are well over 2 metres deep up to the jetty. Wider boats can be moored to the side or, if there is little traffic, alongside. On shore there is a modern version of a privy. There are rubbish bins and a picnic area with wooden tables.

The only thing you can't expect here is a supply of electricity or water, and the Kro

> **TIP**
>
> From the Viking-style shed, a hiking trail leads above the steep coast through a shady beech forest, following the Alsenfjord to an old palace with a beautiful garden and pond.

(inn) mentioned in the guidebook is nowhere to be found. But in the gardens of the few small houses, hydrangeas are fragrant, and one of the residents offers his own honey on a 'trust' table. On the jetty next door, you can visit replicas of old Viking ships; there are information boards and, on land, a Viking-style wooden shed (in the background on the left of the photo).

5 VARNÆS VIG

The Aabenraa Fjord is a magnificent sailing area with deep water and a high forested coastline. Just behind the 24-metre-high steep shore of Varnæs Hoved at the entrance to the fjord, the deep inlet of Varnæs Vig opens up, lined with small forests, meadows and pastures. Here – at the head of the bay – there is a white sandy beach and a jetty extending far into the fjord. The water is up to 2.2 metres deep everywhere; only in strong westerly winds can the water level drop, by up to 1 metre. Even a 50-foot series giant can find room at the jetty. And if you want, you can also anchor without restriction next to the jetty. The harbour fee must be deposited in a postbox at the jetty. It includes electricity, but this is only switched on from 8pm to 8am.

TIP

Take an inflatable boat to the wreck in the middle of the large bay.

Every now and then a few fishermen land their catch, and at the end of the day they meet on the terrace of their thatched wooden huts, where they light a cigarette and toast with a beer. There are rubbish bins, pleasant picnic spots and a toilet that is best avoided – a kind of fixed Portaloo. What to do here? It's a perfect spot to spend a quiet day with the children, because the beautiful beach, the reedy banks and the small bathing jetty are reminiscent of Enid Blyton stories, or *Swallows and Amazons*. The village itself is 2.5 kilometres inland, so there are no facilities in the immediate vicinity.

Varnæs Vig bay at the entrance to the Aabenraa Fjord is an ideal place for swimming.

6 BARSØ ISLAND

Barsø is tiny compared to many of Denmark's 1,419 islands, inhabited by only 22 people who live mainly from agriculture. Fields, meadows, pastures and forests cover the hilly landscape of the quiet farming islet in the Little Belt, which has a kind of steep coast in the north. To the west, the ferry docks – and that is exactly where there is a modern jetty with space for visitors. The shores are green all the way to the water; there are picnic benches on a strip of grass next to the jetty and a beach next to the ferry dock.

On a relaxing walk around Barsø, you pass the oldest house on the islet, built in the 16th century. The exhibition on the island's history in the orangery of an old farmstead should not be missed. But you won't find any shopping facilities or a restaurant. There is room in the harbour for boats with a draught of up to 1.8 metres, but be careful: if you take the bend too far towards the beach, you will soon be stranded. The mooring fee must be deposited in the postbox at the toilet block.

TIP

Plantain grows everywhere on the edges of fields, and has long been used to help treat itching from insect bites and burns.

Only 22 people live on the small island of Barsø.

The private jetty at Stagodde on Haderslev Fjord is a gateway to a peaceful haven with a romantic sandy beach.

7 STAGODDE

Just behind Årøsund, a narrow, buoyed channel leads into Haderslev Fjord. For more than 7 nautical miles, the reed-covered banks jut out into the mainland; the fjord is as narrow as a river, and outside the channel, which has been dredged to a depth of 6 metres, it is shallow enough to run aground. Only at the beginning, on the port side at Stagodde, is there enough water to reach a jetty (up to 2.2 metres depth). Admittedly, this private site is very, very quiet, but there is room for visitors. And those who wander in will find themselves at a well-kept mooring

TIP

Consider a trip to Haderslev – as one old guidebook notes: 'The old town is a rewarding experience even for staunch cockpit-sitters'!

including electricity, water, toilet block, barbecue area and club house. A tiny sandy beach lies romantically between tall reeds. But beware: a few years ago, outboard motors and electronic parts worth six figures were stolen here. Unfortunately, this now happens even in secluded Danish harbours.

8 HEJLSMINDE

If you have no more than 1.6 metres of draught, you can meander through the buoyed fairway into the harbour of Hejlsminde. The place itself is not a jewel, but the harbour has charm and everything your heart desires – from fishing boats to a wooden pool where children can race crabs. Right next door is a wonderfully wide sandy beach with a beach volleyball court, surfboard and SUP rental and child-friendly shallow water. Of course, the typical Danish hot dog stand is not far away, and a little further on there is the restaurant Baade Og, which serves Flammekueche (perhaps more familiar by its French name, tarte flambée) as a speciality. There is also a bicycle hire shop, a grocery shop and a hotel where you can use the swimming pool.

> **TIP**
>
> There is a hiking trail around the Hejlsminde right next to the harbour. The water is separated from the Baltic by a dam and is a bird sanctuary.

9 FØNS VIG

This place is probably known only to a very few insiders, as no map or guidebook provides a description. The small jetty, in the middle of a nature reserve, is set up for visitors and keeps places free. On the jetty there is exactly one electricity connection, a picnic table and a rubbish bin. Thanks to a stone embankment, the site is well protected from the open bay. There are about two dozen berths, and numerous dinghies, fishing boats and anglers moor here. Coming from the sea, access behind the jetty is easier (up to 2.2 metres

The small harbour of Hejlsminde had brand new jetty facilities and sanitary blocks installed in 2019. Volunteers help out every weekend over the winter.

> **TIP**
>
> Head north toward the beach kiosk for a lovely walk along unspoilt beach, past grassy expanses and fields of flowers. There is a small, fairly new harbour house with a toilet, its size restricted to 20 square metres in the interests of nature conservation.

draught and 3.5 metres width possible) if you stick to the starboard side. On the port side, you have to stay close to the pilings, because it quickly becomes shallow behind them.

10 LØVERODDE

Right at the entrance to the Kolding Fjord, behind the sandy outcrop of Løverodde on the southern shore, lies Paradisbugten – and the name says it all, even if the power station on the shore opposite is unfortunately an eyesore. Nevertheless, the three wooden jetties of local sailing and motorboat clubs in the western part of the bay are an invitation to stay for free. Tucked away below the cliff and surrounded by dense forest, these moorings, without electricity or water, are the purest oases of tranquility – with wonderfully small beach niches between green reeds, lawns, barbecue areas, tables, swings and basic toilets.

Now and then, when one of the small freighters pulls towards Kolding, the boats bob in the swell. 'It only gets crowded here at weekends,' said a Danish sailing crew from Fredericia. About 600 metres further east there is a car park, a pleasant bathing beach, rubbish bins and a restaurant. Directly in front of it, another wooden jetty juts out deep into the fjord. 'There is a water depth of up to 7 metres at the bridgehead, and the jetty is now being renovated at a cost of 200,000 euros,' the restaurant's landlord told us in summer 2016.

The jetty at Føns Vig might not be found on any map or handbook but is still worth a visit.

> **TIP**
>
> The Café Løverodde at the jetty is an astonishingly high-quality a la carte restaurant with lunch and dinner menus, open from the beginning of May until the end of August.

11 BREJNING

The mountainous shores of the scenically beautiful Velje Fjord, which reaches almost 15 nautical miles deep into the country, are covered with dense beech forests. Hardly anyone goes there in search of the town of the same name at the head of the fjord, which the guidebook describes as 'somewhat desolate'.

Rarely crowded, Løverodde is an oasis of calm in the Kolding Fjord.

It is rather the many small anchorages and landing places that make the fjord so attractive. One of these is the circular harbour of Brejning halfway along the fjord – a cosy little place with full facilities, including a campfire site, diesel filling station, rental bikes and a modern children's playground with wooden frames. It is located right next to the park of a castle-like estate. And in the harbour, in the few cube-like and wood-clad residential and office buildings next to the clubhouse, there is even an art gallery. A steep climb leads up to the village. A bakery, pizzeria and grocery shop are about a kilometre away.

TIP

The harbour restaurant Galionen, with its terrace directly in front of the moorings, has a remarkable daily changing menu of fish dishes.

12 KORSHAVN

Narrow headlands and hilly peninsulas wind around the north-eastern tip of Funen like a labyrinth. Small islands lie in the shallow water. One of the headlands is shaped like an index finger bent into a hook, and in the middle of it is a sheltered anchorage that is probably one of the most beautiful in the area. On the western shore of this round bay, Odense Sejlklub operates a wooden jetty with wide berths, which also offers space for a modern 50-footer (maximum permissible weight: 12 tonnes). There are a few summer cottages and a hotel in the vicinity. The campsite, with shopping facilities, is 2 kilometres away.

It is the quiet landscape and the unique location that make this natural harbour beautiful to stay in. There is electricity and water at the jetty, a public sanitary facility is 200 metres away, and barbecue and picnic areas, rubbish bins and a self-service counter with the most essential provisions await the sailor ashore. There is a payment machine for mooring fees. A second wooden jetty next door is reserved for fishermen – a good opportunity to buy fresh fish for dinner.

Text: Michael Amme

TIP

A hike in the evening to the steep coastline at Funen offers great views over the area, and across to Sealand and Samsø.

The well-kept harbour of Brejning lies halfway to Vejle. It has all the facilities and an idyllic setting.

4 SOUTH FUNEN ARCHIPELAGO

Sail in the wake of a young couple who set off from Wismar for the Danish South Sea in an H-boat.

The idea was born after the last university lecture during a sundowner sail in Wismar Bay: instead of turning around at Poel as usual, why not sail on to somewhere in the Danish island region? Is that feasible without much experience, or simply a crazy idea?

We've just got our H-boat *Geronimo* as a gift from my father at the beginning of the season. I grew up with the Opti and now I finally have the right boat to get my boyfriend excited about sailing. Sebastian, who grew up in southern Germany and spent his childhood more in the mountains than on the water, is fortunately quickly infected by the sailing bug; parallels to his hobbies of paragliding and kite surfing certainly help. Throughout the whole season, we spend every spare minute on the boat, having fun with sporty sailing so close to the water – including testing the limits of the yacht.

With increasing experience and the approaching semester break, a window of opportunity finally opens for us to look beyond the horizon. What's stopping us? So, we buy waterproof mobile phone cases, install the navigation app, fill two backpacks with clothes

Some of the small islands of South Funen are perfect for overnight camping.

Faaborg

DENMARK

Sønderborg

LANGELAND

ÆRØ

LOLLAND

Langø

Schleimünde

Baltic Sea

FEHMARN

Eckernförde

Lemkenhafen

Kiel

Großenbrode

GERMANY

Neustadt

N

DANISH SOUTH SEA

50 NAUTICAL MILES

Wismar

and food, put the tent, cooker and sleeping bags in the boat, add the kite equipment – and that's it! We plan to head north-west out of Wismar Bay. After all, what better place for sailing than the many sheltered islands of the Danish South Sea?

Being free, camping on uninhabited islands, no problems with too much draught.

Travelling as it used to be, scaled down and close to nature – that is our dream for the summer. At the end of August, just before we set sail, we run some last errands at the outfitters in Wismar. When the owner hears about our plan, he encourages us to sail the 48 kilometres to Großenbrode in one go, given the ideal prevailing wind direction. Actually, we wanted to sail along the coast through the Bay of Lübeck to Fehmarn.

Without further ado, we throw our plans overboard right at the start – and get a first taste of what awaits us out there. In Wismar Bay, the waves quickly become relatively high,

and Sebastian has to work hard for hours on end. But: with the last light of day, we arrive safely in Heiligenhafen. A perfect start.

During the following days, we continue into the Langelandsbelt to the sweet fishing harbour of Langø on Lolland. With the hoisting of the courtesy flag, the locals' opinion of our venture changes in a beat. While on Fehmarn we get sceptical looks and pitying comments from passers-by about our sleeping place under the tarpaulin, the sight of our boat brings a friendly smile to the face of even the toughest Danish fisherman.

We reach the Danish South Sea, via Marstal, five days after the start in Wismar. In fantastic weather we enjoy the finest island hopping. Just as we had dreamed, we don't sleep in a harbour for a week. Instead, we anchor in great bays on tiny islands like Drejø, Strynø and Birkholm. Sometimes we are completely alone, at most encountering a few cows. We explore the islands on foot,

Steering away from the Fehmarnsund Bridge, heading towards Denmark.

spend the afternoon in a cute island café or kite on lonely beaches. In the evening we sit around the campfire in front of the tent with a view of our boat and the sunset over the Baltic Sea. Meanwhile, a simple meal sizzles on the hissing gas cooker. Wonderful days!

Time seems to stand still. On some of the small islands, apart from cafés there are also

self-service shops based on trust: vegetables, fruit and other things are freely available, you take what you need and put the money in the cash box. Dream conditions. But why are we the only dinghy sailors far and wide? The answer comes immediately. When we reach the northernmost destination in Faaborg, the weather changes abruptly and autumn announces itself. The way back is adventurous.

Before we reach Sønderborg, an unpredicted front hits us. Suddenly we have a wave of 1.5 metres and become the plaything of the elements. With only a fraction of our jib we fly sometimes over, sometimes through the waves. Clouds of spray envelop us. A wet, wild ride. We reach Hørup Hav exhausted.

You can sail these waters on a small boat, but don't forget space will be at a premium.

Despite our oilskins, we are soaked through to our underwear, but at least our boat remains intact, and we sit in the harbour, relieved. For the first time we realise the purpose of these facilities as a safe haven. Gratefully, we retreat to a pavilion to escape the rain and sort out our belongings. The inventory shows: not a single pair of dry trousers left in the luggage, the food supplies soaked.

While we are still getting things sorted out, we start talking to two Danes. They are enthusiastic about our trip and tell us old stories of their youth. The jetty beer is on our new friends – it has never tasted so good.

The club members invite us to a pizza supper and let us use their clubhouse and kitchen. This way we can dry all our things without any problems. As the rain and wind abated over the next few days, our enthusiasm for dinghy sailing quickly returned. And also

our determination to bring the boat back to Wismar under sail; in between we had flirted with the idea of a trailer return trip. So off we went to Schleimünde. On the long crossing we philosophise about the first meal we will cook back in Wismar. Food is a constant topic during the long journeys.

During the sometimes eight-hour sailing days, we usually have muesli bars for lunch. Cooking at sea is practically impossible in the dinghy, even at wind force 2. With the tiny gas cooker and no refrigeration, we usually have noodle or rice variations in the evening. Especially in bad weather, a good meal brightens the mood enormously. No sooner have we arrived in Schleimünde than a man appears at the stern, holding a hot pan with a tempting aroma: fried potatoes with onions and bacon! Beaming with joy, he introduces himself as Hartmuth. 'I'm travelling with a

Even on the smaller islands there are things worth seeing, such as this pretty church on Drejø.

Sometimes sailing these waters can be a little too relaxing.

Surprise, an 8-metre keel boat. Even that is a rarity in the harbours. But an H-boat, that tops everything!' He is keen to hear about our trip and invites us on board for roast potatoes and wine. It will be an unforgettable evening.

The last major obstacles on our way back to Wismar turn out to be the military training areas Putlos and Todendorf. Both are used for shooting from 9am to 5pm on weekdays, and as we slowly approach them from the Schlei, we are surprised at how loud the gunfire is. Originally, Sebastian and I had resolved never to sail further than 10 nautical miles from the coast. But that's not possible here, at least not easily.

First, we try to get special permission from the military training centre to cross the firing areas. The Federal Defence officer on the other end of the phone can't believe

our question and laughs at us: 'You want to go through there with a dinghy? You must be crazy!' But finally he tells us about the buoys that we should pass at certain times. Navigationally, this is a real challenge, especially as we lost our compass shortly before the trip. We soon realise: either we wait a week in Laboe for a longer firing break, or we sail around the area, always following the flashing buoys. As the wind is offshore, the waves shouldn't be too high, so we decide to set off on the 65-kilometre violent slog. First 10 nautical miles out into the Baltic Sea.

We have fun, everything goes perfectly. We rush along at 5 to 7 knots. But 5 nautical miles before our turning point, a wind shift to the west surprises us. A huge wave quickly builds up. Soon there are no ships to be seen around us. Only in the distance on the horizon

There are lots of isolated spots to discover on the Danish islands.

do we see a large freighter. A queasy feeling now descends.

At first, we still have everything well under control. But then a wave and a gust come together and the boat starts to slide like crazy. With all the luggage, it reacts sluggishly and can hardly be kept on course. So far out and with the wave, it's a knife-edge ride – if we capsize, we're not sure if we could right it; if we were in any doubt, we'd need to alert emergency services. Whether our mobile phone could still help us then is debatable. Only when the main is recovered do we get the boat under control again. Nevertheless, it is still six hard wet hours to Heiligenhafen. How we wish we had a keel under the hull at this moment.

As if they have sensed our fear, porpoises appear on the crossing. They swim with us for a while and distract us from our worries. You can hardly get any closer to the animals than on a dinghy. Eventually it is done. Totally exhausted, we reach Fehmarn and spend the night on an old shipyard site. We need some time off, so we put the dinghy away for another night at the Bennewitz sailing school in Heiligenhafen. We are warmly welcomed there, and Ralf and his team listen to our stories about the adventures with our *Geronimo*. When we see the Swedish Heads, the carved faces on the dolphins of the approach to Wismar on the day of our return, a feeling of happiness flows through me – and a relief that I have never felt before. Sebastian, too, is the happiest person in the world that day and is now a real sea dog. It was an exciting, but also a magical summer in the South Sea.

Text: Lisa Harms and Sebastian Völkel

5 BIRKHOLM

Entering the cosy harbour of Birkholm.

There is really nothing on Birkholm – except peace, nature and an absolute idyll.

The archipelago of South Funen is very popular with pleasure boaters. Ærø, with its beautiful harbour towns of Marstal and Ærøskøbing, is particularly so. But in summer it is often so lively that the boats moor across the berths in the crowded harbours. Only a few crews stray to Birkholm. It's right next door and one of the smallest inhabited islands in Denmark. However, there's really not much to see or discover on the moraine island. With an area of less than 100 hectares, it is not even as big as Helgoland and its highest point is just 2 metres above sea level. But anyone passing the narrow harbour entrance is invariably overcome by a sense of tranquility: no cars, souvenir shops or restaurants. Instead, you can enjoy unspoilt nature and precious silence.

In the 19th century, more than 80

BIRKHOLM

0.5 NAUTICAL MILES

Birkholm Harbour

A perfect Danish summer – anchoring off the coast, relaxing on the beach and swimming in the cooling waters.

inhabitants lived here and there was even a school in addition to a merchant and a telegraph station. The people engaged in agriculture and fishing. Today there are only five islanders who spend the whole year on the island. The remaining houses in the village serve as summer residences. Nevertheless, the island had its own small newspaper until recently, when it had to be buried along with its former producer and editor. The few remaining inhabitants are known as the 'French of the archipelago' because of their irrepressible sense of humour and their festive mood. They have established a little tradition of giving special nicknames to those who

have mishaps: a newly arrived journalist who ran out of fuel halfway on his speedboat was henceforth called 'Halfway'. Another, who lost control of his cordless screwdriver, was given the name 'Propeller'.

Twice a day the mail boat comes from Marstal, which also serves for the exchange of goods, refuse collection and as a passenger ferry. *Banke banke på* – 'Knock knock, is anyone there?' At its mooring, two boys play at the lovingly decorated miniature house in which is located the pumping station for the island's saltwater toilets. It was built by a German, Heinz, who every year comes to Birkholm several times for a few weeks and

An idyllic view over the island.

does all kinds of repair work in the harbour. Over time, he has earned himself a very special honour: he is allowed to hoist the Dannebrog, the Danish flag, in the morning. At the end of the day, he even gets vocal support from harbour and island residents of all kinds, when classics like Rod Steward's 'Sailing' set the mood for the evening.

Two or three times a day, the fishing brothers Frede and Morten Mortensen enter the harbour. Immediately, someone wakes up from their daydreaming in the hope of grabbing fresh crabs or eel. The two natives are well into their seventies, have spent their whole lives on the island and enjoy cult status in the region. Their catch has made it into Copenhagen's finest restaurants, while their unique mentality has sometimes landed the two of them on international television programmes. The Mortensens have long since been financially secure, but they can't stop

fishing, says Morten: 'For us, it's as much a part of the day as getting up in the morning and having a cup of black coffee.'

His brother, Frede, was also harbourmaster here for 40 years, like their father before him, until Christian, then aged 25, took over this voluntary position. His family has owned a summer house on Birkholm for many years and he enjoys island life, sailing his catamaran and diving. Since the harbour fee is thrown into a box on a trust basis, he has plenty of time for that. Fresh water and a self-service kiosk can be found in the island's community centre, 1 kilometre away. Every morning, Christian's mother bakes bread and cakes, which she sells very cheaply. Ice cream for young and old is always in stock, and sometimes you can find locally made liqueur. Recently, a shower cabin was added next door. A woman with shampoo in her hair peers out while her little daughter runs to the kiosk to get some change: 'You need a few coins,' the mother laughs with a Dutch accent before the hot water continues to flow.

The Danish Larsson family is also moored in the harbour with their boat from Svendborg. In their own words, they are 'addicted to Birkholm' and moor here for a fortnight every year. The season ticket (which includes electricity) is very economical compared to most other harbours. The children love the island and spend several hours a day hunting crabs and crayfish. Red-haired Viktor has renamed the island 'Vores Ø' – 'Our Island'. The day before, they were in Marstal for supplies on the mail boat and are now glad to be 'home' again: 'Much too stressful over there!'

Right next to the harbour basin is a child-friendly, shallow-sloping beach with a view of a seemingly endless procession of passing boats on the Mørkedyb, the shipping channel between the islands of Egholm and Birkholm that connects the western part with the south-eastern part of the shallow island sea. A German sailor from Stade is sailing through the Danish South Sea this summer on his boat *Regentrude*, named after a book by Theodor Storm – a trip in memory of best friend. Six days ago, he came to Birkholm for the first time and immediately fell in love with this corner of the world: the next day, the 25th anniversary of the new harbour was celebrated and the newcomer was immediately invited to be there. Since then, he has extended his stay every day, knows all the faces by now and already has a few anecdotes about the island. Maybe he will continue his journey today. Or maybe not…

Text: Morten Strauch

The flag of Denmark, the Dannebrog, flies over the harbour.

6 SVENDBORGSUND

The view of the southeast entrance to the Sound, from one of the pretty beach houses that line the shore of Troense.

Those who have been here once always return: Svendborg Sound is a desirable evergreen destination, and not just for sailors.

Svendborg Sound is certainly one of the most scenic and varied destinations in the Danish South Sea around Funen. Denmark's best natural harbour is located here, along with many beautiful jetties and a town that offers pure maritime history.

If you ask owners with moorings on the German Baltic coast what their favourite destinations are, where they almost always stay a day or two longer than planned, one name comes up particularly often: Svendborg and the associated sound. It is simply one of those places that is still fun to visit even after the tenth time. Where you always discover something new. It offers something for everyone, whether you're a culture vulture, a pub crawler, a lover of classic yachts and traditional ships, or you relish a shopping spree. And of course there is the location. Like a picturesque river, the sound meanders between the three islands of Funen, Tåsinge and Thurø. It offers wonderful panoramas throughout. The views range from idyllic anchor bays like Thurø Bund to dignified captains' houses in Troense or entire castles such as Valdemars Slot.

At the entrance to Svendborg Sound, Thurø Bund Bay is on the right, Troense on the left.

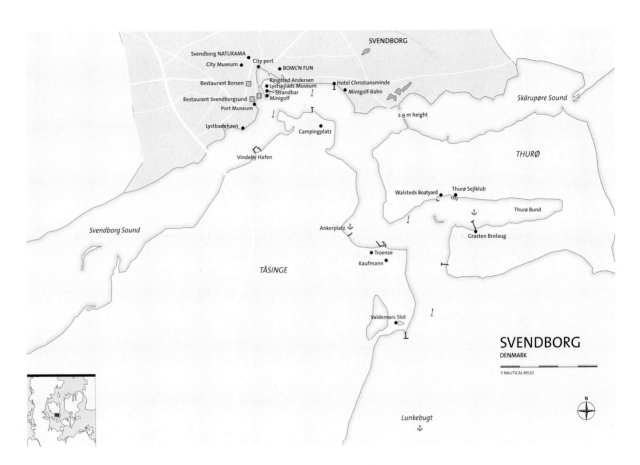

In addition, the place breathes maritime history: still active shipyards and traditional ships in Svendborg and Thurø prove that this is still an epicentre of the sailing scene today. And right in the heart of the city, at the Ring-Andersen shipyard, tall ships of all kinds have been built since the 19th century. The family business, now in its fourth generation, recently celebrated its 150th anniversary.

Louise Ring-Andersen is proud of this, too, as she welcomes us at the shipyard gate in her blue overalls. The young Dane works at the shipyard together with her brother, Jesper, while their father, Peter, still pulls the strings. She knows a lot about the great days of the shipyard. 'My great-great-grandfather Jørgen was famous for his fast schooners, he had learned his trade in Aberdeen, where the

Empire's fast tea clippers were built.' So when he returned to Svendborg, he brought with him the know-how for exceptionally well-made sailing ships and gave them his own personal touch with a clipper-like stern, shaping a kind of 'Svendborg schooner'.

He was one of the first to be granted the right to establish a repair yard on the then tiny island of Frederiksø, which is now connected to the city by bridge. 'The island was actually just a larger shoal, but then grew quite quickly.' The reason for this was that the ballast sand of many ships had to be removed for the repair work. This was simply spread over the island, which slowly grew over the decades. A creative way to expand his premises. During the tour of the shipyard with the likeable Dane, however, the

Rigging the mast of a traditional vessel in the Ring-Andersen shipyard.

12-member shipyard crew is busy with one of the boatbuilders' unloved jobs: they are sawing up an old 20-metre sailboat that was past saving.

No new four-masted schooners have been built for a long time, but Ring-Andersen has made an excellent name for itself as one of the best shipyards for repairs and extensive refits of working ships, and also repairs many traditional ships. This is evidenced by Louise's brother Jesper, who is next door rigging a new mast that the shipyard built from larch for a Danish refit customer. Then she leads the way into a securely locked attic that brings back to life the great days of the schooners: there, the shipyard founders have preserved over a century of figureheads, ornaments and hundreds of sailors' names. The relics of past

seafaring history are everywhere: navigation lamps, compass casings, ancient cork life jackets, the first radio direction finders and much more. A wonderful collection that makes the history of the shipyard visible in one fell swoop.

We want to know if the many nameplates all come from scrapped ships. 'Fortunately not, many of them are from ships that changed owners and were renamed. We often got them as gifts and hung them up here.' If you want to immerse yourself in the era of wooden boatbuilding, you can marvel at beautifully preserved examples not 200 metres away at the museum ships' pier in Svendborg. Traditional ships also meet there every year on a leg of Funen Round, the seasonal highlight for these vessels.

A hundred and fifty years of shipbuilding history can be found here.

Another shipyard visit shows how large Svendborg's fleet once was: above Bettina Walsted's desk hangs a huge panoramic photo of Thurø Bund Bay, completely covered with cargo ships. 'In winter, there were sometimes 130 ships moored here,' she says. Thurø was also the island of captains and shipping companies; many of the houses on land were named after the family's ships and still are. So, if you stumble across houses with names like 'Concordia', you know why that is. But Walsted has made a name for itself in Svendborg for quite different ships: beautiful and fast wooden yachts.

Although new builds have become rare here too, there are great restoration projects almost every year, as the newly appointed shipyard manager Bettina, who has taken over running Walsted with her sister, tells us. In 2018, the famous 115-year-old customs cutter *Kong Bele*, built by the Danish government to hunt smugglers, was refitted. 'The boat had to be as fast as an arrow for that,' says master boatbuilder Henning Bøgh, who runs the workshop for Bettina.

The Walsteds, famous for sailing boats that are hard to beat, were the first choice. Of course, the shipyard also depends on maintenance and work on GRP yachts; hardly any business can survive on wooden yachts alone these days. Even after decades, the two are still enthusiastic about their home territory: 'There are great anchorages, Svendborg is considered one of the harbour towns in Denmark with the best bars, restaurants and many great sailing events. The Classic Regatta

Magnificent rooms and a huge collection of hunting trophies in the 17th-century castle at Valdemars Slot.

TIP

Valdemars Slot is definitely worth a visit. It is about 25 minutes' walk from Troense.

for yachts, Funen Rundt for the traditional sailors, Havet Rundt for the smaller dinghies – there's always something going on here!' says Bøgh. The shipyard's customers obviously see it that way, too, because owners come from as far away as America every summer to sail on the Baltic Sea and leave their yachts behind. Walsteds have the best anchorage in the area right outside their office window: Thurø Bund.

Even today, the yachts are perfectly protected between the beech forest on the south shore and the homesteads and houses of the fishermen and captains on the north shore.

'I've lived here for 50 years, and nothing has ever happened to a boat here in a storm!' says Bøgh.

Today the island is a popular place to live, house prices are high, and those who can afford it live here – or opposite in Troense, the most exclusive residential area in the whole sound. House prices there are easily 25 per cent higher than in Svendborg. The picturesque location makes it so. Thurø Bund is considered Denmark's best natural harbour, and in summer there are often 30, 40 or more yachts moored there. There is room for all of them. But if you only anchor here, you are missing out, says Bøgh, who jumps into the van with us and drives to the small harbour of Thurø Sejlklub where, on the shore, ancient fishing tackle huts with thatched roofs form a picturesque backdrop between huge oak trees. Fish traps hang out to dry, and the club has beautiful picnic areas by the water. Even nicer are the ones on the slope up by the old clubhouse, with a fantastic view of the sound from the terrace.

As a Svendborg Sound fan, you have to moor here at least once. This is also where the boatbuilder himself moors his Hallberg-Rassy 29. And what are his favourite spots for an evening in Svendborg? 'In warm summer weather, the beach club on Frederiksø is just great for a sundowner! And afterwards you can go to the restaurant Svendborgsund at the ferry pier. They still cook really good traditional Danish food, not that new-fangled burger stuff!'

If you sail along the Svendborg Sound from Thyrø towards the city, you will pass the part of the sound where every sailor has probably dreamed of owning a house: Troense. Situated slightly on a slope, the colourful, immaculately restored old houses with their own private jetty and well-tended gardens gleam in all their varied hues. The harbour just inside the bend is perfect for an overnight stop, or just for the popular trip to Valdemars Slot. It used to be a pilgrimage destination for sailors, too, as it was home to the Danish Lystsejlads Museum, a fine collection of wooden dinghies and yachts from Denmark's long sporting tradition. But eventually space simply became too tight, and the exhibition moved to its own rooms in Svendborg. The Renaissance castle of the king's son Valdemar from the 17th century is nevertheless worth a visit.

One of the best places in harbour on the island of Frederiksø is the Strandbar, near the Kammerateriet.

The splendour of the king's hall, the dining room, the historically preserved bedchambers, the gigantic collection of trophies from the passionate hunters in the family of the present owners – all this provides an impression of what it was like to live here once as crown prince. The jobs that the estate brought ensured that a small village formed around it, now in ruins. Troense, right on the waterfront, was built later when Svendborg's shipbuilding and trade boomed in the 18th and 19th centuries.

At Troense, and after just outside Svendborg, the sound is at its narrowest, with the most current. The waters can be challenging. If you want to understand the weather conditions in the sound, it is best to talk to the harbourmaster of Svendborg, Joacim Bøllehuus. He has sailed the sound for years as skipper of the historic ferry *Helge*, 100 days a year. 'The current is of course an issue here, it can be around 3.5 knots. If the wind has been blowing strongly from the south-east and then turns to the west and dies down, the water sloshes back into the Baltic Sea like in a bathtub.' If, on the other hand, the wind blows from the west for a long time, the water level can drop by 1.2 metres and then surprise sailors, for example off Troense, by sticking their keel in the mud. 'But actually, there are very few problems, the shallows are well buoyed.'

During his time as skipper of the *Helge*, he got to know the sound in all its facets. Every day is different here, he says, especially in spring, when early morning fog often forms over the cold water and renders the sound magical. 'You also see a lot of animals here, for example sea eagles over Tåsinge. Sometimes you can also see seals and dolphins. In 2015, two very

Umbrellas adorn the old town on Kyseborg Street.

Sailing with a view past fancy old homesteads in the narrows of the Sound between Thurø and Troense.

large dolphins, at least 3 metres long, got lost in the sound when they followed the shoals of herring. They swam here repeatedly for a week, so every trip with the *Helge* was a big dolphin show!' The ferry, built in 1924 at Ring-Andersen, is an institution in the sound. For generations of residents, it has been a school bus, a taxi and a means of transport. Some locals love the boat so much that they have married on it or rent it for private parties after hours.

Among some sailors, however, the boat enjoys a different reputation. 'They called her "Evil Helge" because some of the ferry captains didn't always avoid the sailors. There was also some pretty loud abuse from some crews,' says Joacim Bøllehuus. 'They believe that a ship operating under power must always

avoid sailors. But the collision prevention rules are clear: if a course change is not possible in narrow, shallow waters, the sailor must also take evasive action – many just don't know that any more because their training was a long time ago!'

Ask the harbourmaster of Svendborg about his favourite places to go out in the city and he'll tell you straight away: 'To the Strandlyst for a beer and to the Børsen for dinner. These are really nice maritime pubs. Ask the landlord Lauri there for his best stories, he can tell the most amazing tales!'

But we have an appointment with another character from Svendborg: Ole Ingemann Nielsen. The Dane with the mischievous grin, who is constantly gesticulating across the

65

piers with his mobile phone glued to his ear, is always on duty: if not as a project developer, then for his second passion: the Silverrudder single-handed race. It takes place in mid to late September and in just six years has become a success story that has left everyone in the sailing scene speechless. The idea came from the editor of the Danish sailing magazine *Badnyt*, Morten Brandt-Rasmussen, in 2012. Single-handed. Non-stop. Around the island of Funen – sorted.

'I was immediately enthusiastic and proposed it to my sailing club. Many said: Ole, that's a crazy idea, no one will come!' laughs the Dane today. In fact, only 13 starters took to the course in 2012, and by no means all of them finished. Typical for the race, sometimes the skippers struggle with long lulls, sometimes with too much wind. 'But then the whole

thing went through the roof! The next year 100 skippers came and then 100 more every year! We had to limit the starting field to 450 participants, we can't handle any more. This year the starting places were sold out after a few hours!'

The race today is a huge happening, the whole city joins in, the city harbour is reserved for the participating boats in the 38th calendar week. There will be match races, a children's programme, live music and, of course, a big party before and after the start. The event has been a big hit with French and German visitors, and television will probably be here too, says Ole Ingemann, beaming. He attributes the success to the format and the skippers: 'It's a challenge, but it's not such a huge project as crossing the Atlantic, and on top of that it's right on our doorstep. It's just the thing for

The Børsen restaurant is a popular meeting place for sailors.

Every sailor visiting Svendborg Sound should moor at the small harbour of Thurø Sejlklub at least once.

experienced sailors, because that's who most of the people who take part are.'

The event has grown so big that it eats up a lot of the lively organiser's free time. He invests almost 500 hours in the project – every year. Sometimes he doesn't have enough time to sail his own boat, a Sagitta 35, on his local sound. That's why this year he has categorically moved his lunch break to his boat: he and his wife then cook their meal on the gas cooker.

Moreover, the project has unexpected pitfalls: last year, when almost 200 participants did not reach the finish line because of tough slack water, he was left with 200 'finisher' T-shirts. 'But we definitely didn't want them to somehow end up in circulation in a roundabout way, we want it to remain something special!' So now half his sailing club polishes their hulls with cut-up 'finisher' T-shirts in winter.

TIP

Explore Thurø Sejlklub, the most beautiful harbour in the Thurø Bund. A great historical photo of the bay featuring many old schooners hangs on the wall of the fisherman's hut on the far right.

The bundle of energy also knows a lot about his home town, in whose waters he has been sailing for decades. 'Svendborg has always been a lively, modern city. We have a big school with 1,000 high school students, a maritime school for professional sailing.' The town and municipality are doing well, partly because one of the town's great sons gives generous financial support to projects: A.P. Møller, owner of the Møller-Mærsk shipping company, is from Svendborg. Many people here are proud of him; he supports his home region to the best of his ability. Ole Ingemann can fully understand that: for him, the sound is his dream place to this very day. 'It's great here because you can sail in any weather, it's so sheltered. And there are so many great little islands right on your doorstep!'

His favourite is Birkholm, he says, where everything is quiet and there is no fuss, ideal for escaping the stress of a job and organising a regatta. In fact, the sound has an extraordinary amount of activity, largely because the people of Svendborg know how to organise and celebrate festivals so well. Regattas, classical music concerts, music festivals, the largest regional culinary event, the cinema festival in the middle of the harbour that you can visit by boat – the locals are considered very creative in dreaming up new seasonal highlights. Anyone who visits the tourist information

office in the old 'Pakhus' warehouse at the ferry port can see that immediately. Anja Mia Haas runs the office and knows everyone and everything in the town. She talks about the highlights that some sailors discover only by chance. For example, the Kulinarisch Südfünen festival, which takes place in June. That's when regional producers who are Slow Food devotees meet and present their products. 'The range is huge, there are local jam makers, beer brewers, cheese makers, chocolate makers, gin distilleries – people in the region are very creative!' Some products are available in the information office shop, always worth a visit.

As is often the case in Denmark, the events are concentrated in the summer, but there are always original events in the off-season as well. For example, the Aebleraes. During the apple harvest in October, old wooden

Historic thatched-roof fishermen's huts in front of the Thurø Sailing Club marina, one of the most beautiful harbours in the Sound.

The harbour master of Troense is much loved by sailors.

boats loaded with tons of fruit traditionally sail from Rudkøbing, with a stop in Troense, to Svendborg, where they are sold directly from the boat. On land, meanwhile, a folk festival is held around the apple. There is everything that can be made from the raw material: apple pie, apple pancakes, cider, jellies, calvados and whatever else can be dreamed up.

If you want to be closer to sailing, drop by the Danish Lystsejladsmuseum, roughly translated as the museum of recreational sailing, on the old shipyard island of Frederiksø. Founded in the 1990s by a few wooden-boat enthusiasts who, after a restoration, thought it belonged in a museum, the collection now includes around 120 boats, from Paul Elvstrom's Olympic dinghy to Folkboats and classic yachts. 'We want to offer visitors as broad a cross-section as possible of all facets of sailing in Denmark,' says Martin Stockholm, a member of the museum's board of directors. Among them are amazing stories like that of Svend Billesbølle, who sailed around the world in his tiny 18-foot Spidsgatter *Stormy* without making a big fuss about it – hardly conceivable in Facebook and Instagram times. It's stories like this that Svendborg Sound is always good for. Every time you come back here, you discover a new one, for decades. Thank goodness.

Text: Andreas Fritsch

7 SMÅLAND FAIRWAY

Small islands, shallow sounds: the quiet Småland fairway is an idyll in slumber.

There are many destinations in Denmark. Copenhagen, of course, the capital on the Øresund. Anholt and the Danish sunny island of Bornholm, where Siegfried Lenz's 2016 'Schweigeminute' [A Minute's Silence] was filmed. And of course, Ærø with its various small neighbouring islands in the Danish South Sea. All well and good, but those sailing north from the German Baltic coast have another alternative: they can let themselves be blown by a breeze between Langeland and Lolland and then head east. Into the Småland fairway.

A signpost on the small islet of Skalø, which is connected to Fejø by a narrow dike.

What is called a fairway is more like a bay, about 20 by 30 nautical miles in size and framed by several islands. To the north and east Zealand, to the south Falster and Lolland. With coasts that rise flat out of the water. With enchanting places and small harbours. With sounds, passages and a dozen islands and islets all around. The Småland fairway seems a little like it is trapped in a slumber. Most sailors leave it be and sail across it. Why is that? Perhaps because neighbouring Ærø has a world-famous seafaring town, Marstal? Or are there simply too few attractive destinations in the Småland fairway? Is the area too shallow in the end or problematic from a navigational point of view?

We want to find out and start with Skælskør, a small town on Zealand at the entrance to the Småland fairway. The red-brick church rises out of a small sea of houses, and Win Melchers has moored his Compromis 888 *Sebulon* at a wooden floating jetty in the town harbour. 'We're moored in Kiel and on our way to Copenhagen,' he says in the evening, adding, 'This is a good opportunity to have a look at the Småland fairway on the way there.' Then the seventysomething tells of the approach the previous afternoon. 'Dozens of buoys mark the fairway in the almost 3-nautical-mile-long fjord up to here. It really is very idyllic. But right next to the buoys it is very shallow,' says the skipper. The guidebook speaks of a complicated approach, but the advantage, according to

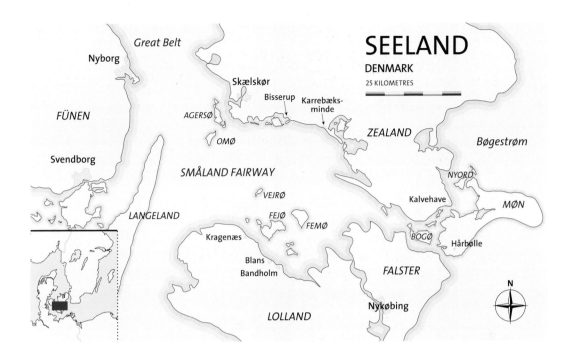

author Jan Werner, is that 'you can always find a place here'.

In front of the Fiskehuset [fish market] at the harbour, red and white Danish flags flap in the wind. Fresh garfish and cod are for sale. A little further on, between red wooden sheds and colourful fishing crates, a smoker oven glows. On the shore, countless fish traps and nets hang stretched over wooden poles to dry in the sun. Two old fishermen in rubber boots pluck rubbish from their meshes. Win Melchers lets his eyes wander over the scenery and says: 'Really beautiful here. But we definitely want to go to the small islands, too!' There are more than a dozen of them in the area, six of which have a harbour and can also be reached with a keel yacht. If you add the dozen harbours and moorings on the coasts and others on the adjacent fairways around Møn and Falster, it quickly becomes clear: there is no shortage of destinations here. The easiest way to reach the area in the west is from the Great Belt.

The water is deep enough everywhere, the current moderate – ideal for those approaching from Flensburg, Kiel or Heiligenhafen. If, on the other hand, you are coming from Rügen or Rostock or want to leave the Småland fairway in the direction of Copenhagen, you will find three more approaches in the south and east of the area: narrow sounds that certainly have their pitfalls. Guldborgsund in the south, for example, can only be navigated by shallow-draught vessels: the nautical chart shows shallows of up to 1.3 metres in the shipping channel! In contrast, the Grønsund between Falster and Møn is at least 5 metres deep. But be careful, in strong winds the water is forced through the narrows at speeds of up to 6 knots. That leaves the approach through Bøgestrøm, ideal for the way to or from Copenhagen. The nominal depth there is 2 metres, but strong westerly winds can reduce the water level.

Just opposite Skælskør is the island of Agersø. The sound between them is less than

An old wooden boat comes out of the water in Omø harbour.

view of the Great Belt, where white ferries and big ships sail. There are many such quiet and dreamy islands in the Småland fairway.

Agersø's neighbouring island Omø is one of them, at least in the off-season. In high summer, as Jan Werner writes in his sailing guide, up to 4,500 sailors head for the island. Then yachts are packed with fishing boats in the small harbour, and the holidaymakers swarm there. They might stop at wooden roadside displays, with homemade jam and apple juice, potatoes and courgettes that you can take home for a few kroner. Or explore the village of Omø By in the centre of the island.

Before heading for the next islands, it's worth taking a look at some beautiful places on Zealand's southern coast. Bisserup, for example, which the Kiel sailor Win Melchers considers an insider tip. 'A tiny harbour, unspoilt and with a sandy bathing beach, a real treasure. That's what sailing was like 50 years ago,' he says. And contrary to what some harbour guidebooks would have you believe, Bisserup is easy to navigate, says Melchers, 'the approach is buoyed, and there are bearing marks and bearing lights'. Karrebæksminde, with its steel bridge and the best bathing beach for miles around, is also worth a stop. Or Vordingborg with its 600-year-old Goose Tower. If you set sail from there for the 15 nautical miles to the islands in the south of the area, you'll find plenty of open water.

2 nautical miles wide, and with a water depth of 57 metres it is one of the deepest places in the western Baltic Sea. Behind it, the islet rises out of the water, pancake-flat, with a small harbour. Fishing boats rock in the waves; here and there someone sorts through his catch. Nearby, sailors picnic at the red wooden tables in the setting sun.

Agersø is peaceful and quiet; the colourful little houses and farms are lined up around the village pond, there is a baker and a grocery shop. The pride of the 174 inhabitants is Agersø Mill, built in 1892, which can be visited in summer. And if you grab a bicycle at the harbour for a small fee, you should cycle to the southern end of the island. You will pass cannons that remind you that Agersø played an important role in the Gunboat War of 1807 to 1814, between Denmark–Norway and the British. Finally, at the Helleholm lighthouse, you have a great

Long cruises are possible, unlike in the narrow channels of the South Funen Archipelago. There are shoals and narrow, buoyed approaches to harbours that require careful navigation, especially as there are extensive flats around the islands and off the coasts. Otherwise, however, the open and wide bay of the Småland fairway is anywhere between 5 and 15 metres deep. And away from the sounds, no one need expect a significant current. The first island on the way south is Vejrø, a little paradise. 'Yes, it's a beautiful place,' says Susanne Bang, manager of the only hotel, smiling pensively. Then she raves about the small island floating in the sea between Zealand and Lolland. It has belonged to the Danish banker Kim Fournais for years.

'He had the harbour dredged and the jetties renovated,' says the young harbourmaster, Mark Harrop Hansen. 'Fournais had picnic tables and benches put up and barbecue areas set up, then the houses were repaired.' First the

one not far from the harbour, now the Skipperly, where you can buy rolls and barbecue meat. Then came the sanitary facilities for the sailors: 'They are like in a four-star hotel,' says the owner of the sailing yacht *Sir Henry*, which is currently moored in the small harbour, 'really great'. He is not bothered by the fact that the mooring fees are considerably higher than in other Danish harbours, 'given the offer! After all, a lot is included in the price, the bikes, the boules court and the tennis court, for example.' And: you can explore the rest of the enchanting island.

First the area around the Skipperly, with the XXL-sized children's playground and the lovingly

The lighthouse marks the western tip of Omø and guides sailors into the Great Belt.

designed rabbit and chicken enclosures. Then the almost untouched nature of Vejrø. The air smells of sea, meadow and forest, you can hear the sea and the poplars. 'Why don't you cycle all the way around?' says Susanne Bang, pointing to the mountain bikes parked at Skipperly. To the south-east of Vejrø are Fejø and Femø, where you should also moor. On Fejø, the largest of the islands in the Småland fairway, to taste the island's own apple juice and visit the two villages of Østerby and Vesterby with their old thatched houses. Björn Schilling from Fehmarn is currently moored in the harbour of Fejø with his Dufour 31. He knows the island from previous cruises and thinks 'it's so beautifully isolated here, that's why I always come back!'

It is also isolated on hilly Femø, at least for those who haven't travelled to the island for the two big events – the Femø Jazz Festival (first weekend in August) or the Femø Women's Camp (eight weeks long in summer). Away from these events, Femø is idyllic – in the two villages where the 120 or so inhabitants live, on the banks of the little river Bækkenet, which runs right through the island, and on the bathing beaches. We return to the coastal strips of the large islands around the Småland fairway, now on Lolland's north coast. There, too, are exciting destinations, such as Kragenæs, Blans and Bandholm. In Kragenæs, you should take time to visit Kong Svends Høj, one of the famous Danish megalithic tombs. In Bandholm is Knuthenborg Safari Park, the largest in Northern Europe. Visitors can see free-roaming herds of zebras, rhinos, giraffes and water buffalo.

Sailing in Ulvsund near Kalvehave. It is not far to Copenhagen from here.

Camels, zebras and rhinos all call Knuthenborg Safari Park near Bandholm on Lolland their home.

Further east, there are even more destinations to choose from. There, the Småland fairway is connected to the Baltic Sea via sounds and inlets. Guldborgsund, for example, is navigable for deep-draught vessels as far as Nykøbing. The two islands of Falster and Lolland lie very close together, and the waterway winds like a river through the mostly isolated and forested landscape. Nykøbing itself, with its 13,000 inhabitants, has an urban feel, with moorings in front of modern four-storey houses in a new residential complex on the waterfront.

Grønsund also has its charms. The small harbour on Bogø, for example, is shared by sailors and the vintage ferry *Ida*, which still operates on the historic route to Stubbekøbing despite the land connection. But the most beautiful place is Hårbølle, a quiet spot on Møn's south coast, with a fish snack bar at the harbour, a summer house settlement and a small grocery shop.

Win Melchers leaves the Småland fairway on his way to Copenhagen via Ulvsund and

The windmill in Østerby on Fejø, the largest island in the Småland fairway.

A fishing boat bobs in the harbour entrance to Bisserup on the south coast of Zealand.

Bøgestrøm. He heads for the harbour of Kalvehave, where the breakwater juts out on to the narrow fairway. It is particularly idyllic a little further on in the tiny harbour of the mini island of Nyord. There are jetties without any creature comforts, but which are situated in a picture-book setting, surrounded by huge marsh meadows that are resting and nesting places for countless bird species.

In addition to the tranquil and atmospheric surroundings, the island has a long seafaring tradition. Or rather, a piloting tradition. For centuries, land ownership on Nyord was associated with the obligation to guide the many ships through the shallow waters between Møn and Zealand. Today, the tiny

pilot lookout Møllenstangen in a cornfield next to the harbour has an exhibition to remind us of those times. It is the smallest museum in Denmark.

The Café Noorbohandelen in the centre of the pretty town above the harbour is also curious. The café is also an off-licence, with a selection that is hard to find even in European cities. Cognac, whisky and grappa specialities from all over the world are on offer, as well as schnapps made from fruits and herbs from the island. From Nyord, it is another 50 nautical miles to Copenhagen for Melchers. Was it the right decision to explore the Smålands fairway on the way to the Danish capital?

'Absolutely,' he says, 'it's incredibly relaxed

here.' He praises the friendly harbourmasters and bridge attendants, sums up that the sanitary facilities everywhere are exceptionally well maintained and is enthusiastic about the fact that in the Smålands fairway there is no daily stress about finding a mooring, at least outside the Danish school holidays. 'You can set sail in the morning and find a berth in the harbour of your choice in the afternoon. And God knows that's not the case in all Danish waters.

Text: Michael Amme

The liquor store in Nyord is well-known for its selection of excellent whiskeys.

The bascule bridge in Karrebæksminde on the south coast of Zealand. Beyond is a large shallow fjord.

8 MØN

The picturesque view over the Baltic Sea from the chalk cliffs of Dronningestolen.

Landmark, foundation and vantage point: the chalk cliffs of Møn are a spectacular destination on the Baltic Sea.

The sky and the sea are separated by 500 steps: that's how high the chalk cliffs of Dronningestolen rise above the narrow beach, 128 metres, dizzyingly steep and dazzlingly white in the sunlight. The view from their green crown stretches in a wide semicircle from north to south across the Baltic Sea. The ferry port in Trelleborg, Sweden, the Dornbusch on Hiddensee and Darßer Ort on the German side – each about 50 kilometres away – all lie just outside the circle of vision below the empty horizon. A truly worthy location for the 'Queen's Chair' – and certainly the most impressive piece of Denmark's short, jagged coastline.

Møns Klint shapes the landscape of the island of the same name in a unique way.

For centuries, its immense wall served as an important landmark for shipping in the Baltic Sea. Later, the wild formations, rising like frozen waves shaped by water, wind and frost, began to exert an attraction on land as well: first came the artists, then the holidaymakers. A few at first, then more and more. Today, the 'foundations of Denmark', whose 70-million-year-old limestone is so spectacularly exposed here, are listed as a UNESCO biosphere reserve.

An open window into the geological past, embedded in magnificent nature. A visit to the nearby harbour of Klintholm is doubly worthwhile for pleasure boat skippers, not only because Møns Klint with its visitor centre is easily accessible from here, but also

Sailing in Bøgestrøm between Møn and Zealand.

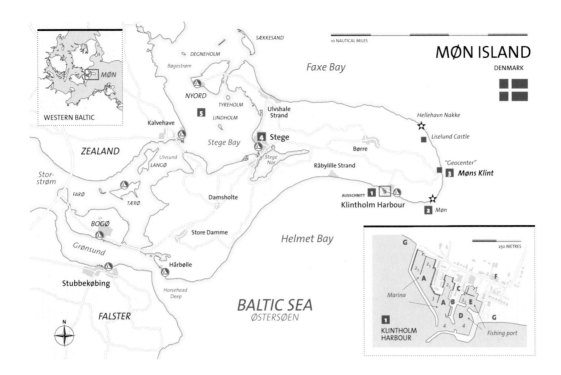

because the town in the south-east of the island offers visitors on their own boat not only a comprehensive nautical and tourist infrastructure, but also the best conditions for summer recreation. If you want to spend more time in the area, you can sail around Møn and get to know its 'other sides' – for example, the flat, sheltered sounds in the north, the small neighbouring island of Nyord, characterised by salt marshes and bird-breeding areas, or the main town of Stege with its 4,000 inhabitants, if you long for the 'big city' again after so much nature...

1 KLINTHOLM HAVN

No other Danish harbour is so centrally located and close to the open Baltic Sea – the perfect staging post on passages to the Øresund and the Swedish south coast. But Klintholm Havn is also a standard stop on cruises through the Småland fairway, which connects the islands of Lolland, Falster, Sjælland and Møn. Approach its illuminated entrance from the south-west. Watch out for nets! There are jetties for visitors in the western and front part of the middle basin (A). Here you can moor in pile moorings or alongside, well protected in the middle of a modern holiday complex. Electricity and water are available. The harbour office (payment machine, opening hours for further requests: 8–9am and 4–6pm) is centrally located (B). The diesel filling station is also located there. Three sanitary buildings are spaced around the harbour. Once you have paid your mooring fee, you can soak up the relaxed atmosphere from the terrace of the Pier to Heaven bar (C). The outer and inner fishing harbours (D and E respectively) are still reserved for cutters and traditional ships. However, large yachts can also be accommodated here by arrangement with the harbourmaster. The sandy beaches (G) flanking the harbour round off Klintholm's 'wellness offer'.

The 'Pier to Heaven' bar in the harbour of Klintholm.

2 MØN FYR

East of Klintholm Havn, the coast begins to rise slowly but steadily. The relatively inconspicuous yellow tower of the lighthouse in the far south-east of Møn takes advantage of the cliffs, which are 10 metres high here. Its identification is Fl(4) W 30s.

3 MØNS KLINT

The central point of contact for exploring Møns Klint and the rest of the biosphere reserve on the Klintholm peninsula is the visitor centre of the GeoCenter, an interactive experience exhibition worth seeing about the natural history of the chalk coast and the densely forested nature reserve inland behind it (opening hours:

between 10am and 6pm, depending on the season). Dronningestolen cliff is only about 300 metres from the car park.

A number of hiking routes start here through the forest area of Klinteskoven to various viewpoints and to the park of Liselund in the north, Denmark's smallest 'castle'. A total of six stairways, spread over almost 7 kilometres of coastline, connect the beach and the cliff edge. By on-board bicycle, the distance from Klintholm Havn to the GeoCenter is about 7 kilometres. There is also a direct bus connection from the end of April to the end of September: Line 678 runs hourly from 10am to 5pm between the harbour and the visitor centre.

The church of Elmelunde.

4 STEGE

This is the main town on Møn, and the supply situation is correspondingly good. Shops and banks can be found along the Storegade, as well as a variety of restaurants. There are visitor berths either in the somewhat industrial Sukkerhavn on the west side of the sound (which is also called the outer harbour seaward of the road bridge), in the Kulhavn opposite or in the basin of the Lystbådehavns, also on the east shore. The harbour office with a payment machine is also on this side. There are four supermarkets to choose from in the immediate vicinity.

Text: Christian Tiedt

Klintholm beach.

9 ARCHIPELAGO SAILING

There are a few things to keep in mind in the Scandinavian archipelago. With these pointers, you can enjoy a wonderful sail through the incomparable rocky landscape.

Refer to charts, but always maintain a careful watch too.

Those who sail in the Scandinavian archipelago for the first time get to know a special area that is unique in the literal sense of the word – there is no other place like it in the world. It is a gigantic labyrinth of waterways between mostly smooth and slightly rounded rocks and islands. It was formed during the last ice age: the ice moved southwards, abrading and shaping the underlying stones. The ice disappeared; the stones remained.

Today, they form a charming, sheltered, varied but also challenging sailing area that stretches from Finland in the east to Sweden in the middle and Norway in the west. The islands are of very different sizes and types. Some are desolate and barren, others are covered with lush green coniferous forests and dotted with the characteristic oxblood-red wooden huts.

Once you have mastered the sometimes treacherous navigation between the thousands and thousands of islets, an archipelago full of charming anchorages and natural harbours opens up. Of course, there are several well-developed marinas of a high standard, but there are also options elsewhere, and the special thing about this area is the magnificent moorings in nature. This is where the majority of sailors come during the Scandinavian summer with its bright nights – into this enchanting world of small waterways, idyllic bays and impressive rock formations.

It almost goes without saying that sailing in this special area only works according to special rules. For example, you moor with the bow on a post. Or a kummel. This is a sea mark that is only found in the archipelago. It may sound rather complicated, but it's really not. However, a skipper has to deal with the subject, he has to know the peculiarities of the area and abide by the rules. There's a saying among sailors: you have to work your way around the archipelago. That's true. But the effort is not too great: as cruising guides for the area make clear, much is self-explanatory. And it is definitely worth it. Every sailor's heart leaps when their yacht bobs alone on

a rock in the glow of the barely setting sun in the stony wilderness.

NAVIGATION

Navigation in the archipelago is demanding. A small lapse in concentration can lead to a collision with a rock under water. At speeds of

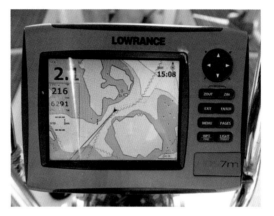

Caution is advisable in narrow channels, but a plotter can be useful to keep track of hazards.

Lighthouses are often smaller here, and their beacons don't carry as far.

The famous Kummel of Päskallavik.

more than 3 knots, the boat is usually seriously damaged. At speeds above 6 knots, you can assume the result will be a total loss.

This makes it all the more important to know exactly where you are at all times. But as charming as the landscape is, it looks the same everywhere. This makes orientation difficult, and it has proved useful to tick off or mark each passed buoy on the map. A simple Post-it is sufficient for this. Alternatively, you can navigate with electronic nautical charts – where you can always see your position immediately.

Using charts, cruising guides and aerial photographs makes sense when navigating.

In very narrow waters, however, this should be done with caution, as a small inaccuracy in the GPS signal can have dire consequences.

LIGHTHOUSES

The lighthouses in Scandinavia are much smaller than in other sea areas. It is not uncommon to need binoculars to locate one. In addition, the range of the beacons is very small. For this reason, night cruising should be avoided altogether in these waters. However, this is not much of a challenge, as it's light for such a long time in the far north during the summer months anyway.

SPECIAL SEA MARKS

Distinctive places in the archipelago are marked with so-called kummels or coloured marks. These are, for example, at places where two fairways cross or where side fairways depart. Kummels are larger, colourfully marked piles of stones, and which are also marked on the nautical chart. The most famous kummel is in the eastern Swedish archipelago at the harbour of Päskallavik. It is a painted wooden figure.

NAVIGATION MARKS

Navigation marks are often used both in the fairways through the labyrinth of the archipelago and when approaching natural harbours and anchorages in narrow bays. As with a leading light, the upper and lower marks must be aligned – then the safe route is clear. In natural harbours in particular, these marks are often simply rectangular spots painted on the rocks.

CRUISING GUIDES AND PILOT BOOKS

There are various manuals describing the area. Those that contain aerial photographs of the

If the weather is stable and not expected to change soon, it is best to lie in the lee of a skerry.

individual bays are particularly suitable for approaching and mooring in natural harbours. In the best books, the aerial photographs are supplemented by depth contours and marked shoals. This allows a relatively simple approach. For Norway and Sweden, for example, such books are available under the name 'Hamnguiden' or 'Tre Veckor' from the Svenska Kryssarklubben.

NATURAL HARBOURS

Mooring in natural harbours should only be done when the weather is stable and no strong wind shifts are expected, as the bays are rarely protected against winds from all directions. Moor with the bow on a skerry in places with offshore wind. This is important because then no swell can develop and the yacht is kept off

the rocks on its leeward side by the wind. The bow lines are fastened with an archipelago anchor (see below), while the stern anchor holds the ship aft.

MOORING AIDS

There are two ways of mooring to the skerries, using either eyebolts/rings set permanently into the rocks and marked, or an archipelago anchor, which must be carried on every yacht. These are available in chandleries, costing about €8 each; you can also find them online. They come in two forms: straight or angled. The straight type are hammered into vertical rock crevices, the angled ones into horizontal crevices. When hammering in, the pitch must always be higher, otherwise the anchor will not hold. The anchors can be loosened by hammering them sideways.

When mooring, use stern anchors and lie with the bow towards the rocks.

STERN ANCHOR

The yacht is held aft in natural harbours by the stern anchor. There are various options – in Scandinavia, the M anchor (aka the Bruce anchor) is widely used. For the duration of the stay in the archipelago, it is permanently attached to the stern or in the stern locker. There should also be 40 metres of line on board. Most skippers use a reel with strap and a 5–10-metre chain attachment for this purpose.

MANOEUVRE

Once a suitable berth has been identified, the mooring manoeuvre can begin. One person stands on the bow, observes the water surface and indicates the distance to the shore by means of hand signals. Depending on the water depth, the anchor is dropped about two to four boat lengths from the shore. The boat slowly approaches the shore. The bow lines are tied to the bow cleat on each side. One of them is

taken ashore by the person on the foredeck. The helmsman stops, sets the stern anchor lightly and then helps at the bow to fasten the archipelago anchors and set the lines. When everything is ready, remember to put the stern anchor through. Important: if possible, set all mooring lines to slip. This allows you to cast off quickly in an emergency – for example, in the event of an unexpected wind shift (if in doubt, sacrifice the archipelago anchors).

BOW LADDER

A bow ladder makes it much easier to get on and off the boat, especially in this area. The most common type, available in specialist shops, are hooked into the bow pulpit or anchor. On some boats, the bow anchor can also be used as a step.

MOORING LINES

In some natural harbours it is necessary to lay mooring lines from the stern to the opposite shore; many skippers do this. In case another vessel is blocked from leaving the bay by the mooring line, there is an unwritten law: only lines that sink to the bottom when cast must be used – so, no floating lines. If possible, these lines are also set to slip so that they can be removed quickly if necessary.

MOORING ALONGSIDE

Occasionally, it is possible to moor alongside the skerry. However, this is the exception rather than the rule and you should only do this if you are sure that no swell runs into the bay. Otherwise the yacht can hit the rocks badly. Extensive fendering is always essential.

MOORING FEES

There is sometimes no harbourmaster in smaller bays or harbours, so it is your responsibility to pay the mooring fee. Usually, a postbox is used as a cash box, into which you post an envelope with the name of the boat and the appropriate amount.

USE OF BUOYS

In Sweden, some bays have buoys from the Svenska Kryssarklubben, the national sailing association. These buoys are free to use, but members may have priority.

FIRE

Sitting on the sun-warmed skerry in the evening and relaxing and barbecuing is widespread and part of the Scandinavian way of life. While barbecuing is not a problem, campfires are frowned upon. The high heat causes the

stones to crack, and water enters these cracks and freezes in winter. Then it literally blows the stones apart.

WASTE DISPOSAL

Occasionally, on popular islands and in natural harbours, waste can be disposed of in specially designed wooden buildings. In all other cases, the rule is that everyone takes away whatever they brought in. Toilets can be found on several islands. These are basic privies. After using them, it is good manners to throw in some sawdust or sand; both are available in sacks. The use of on-board WCs with seawater outlets is prohibited in Scandinavia. Holding tanks are compulsory.

SEA SPRAY HAZARD

When it rains or sea spray flies over the skerry, caution is advised: the round and lovely-looking stones are suddenly as smooth as glass. If you slip, you can fall hard and seriously injure yourself. It is therefore advisable to move carefully, even in non-slip shoes, and not to stray too far from the boat if rain is expected.

Sönke Roever

You will find the occasional hut where you can dispose of rubbish but otherwise take everything away with you.

Narrow passages like this one in Kyrkesund are one
of the attractions of the area.

10 WEST COAST OF SWEDEN

From Marstrand to Smögen, the Swedish archipelago north of Gothenburg is the promised land for 'rock' fans.

1 KUNGSHAMN/HASSELÖSUND

The glaciers of the last ice age formed the rocks of the Swedish west coast – a labyrinth of skerries and islands of smoothly polished granite, separated by sheltered and navigable waterways. Some of these passages are real traffic arteries because of their central location. Hasselösund near Kungshamn, for example, connects the southern and northern parts of Bohuslän.

MOORINGS

South of the bridge in Kungshamn harbour or north in Hasselösund on the island of Smögen.

The view southwards to Hasselösund from the 35m-high Smögenbron. On the right is the village of Smögen, with the island of Hållø in the background.

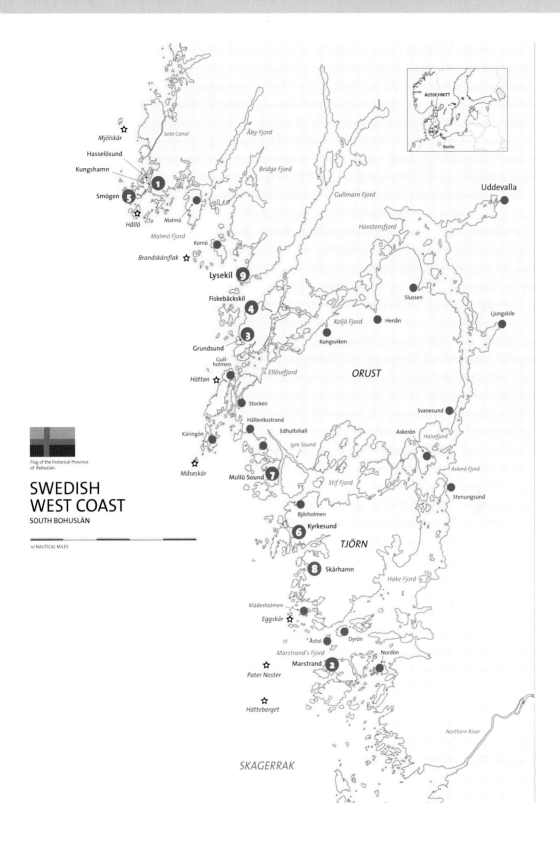

Mjölskär

Hasselösund

Kungshamn

Smögen **5**

Hållö

Malmö

1

Sote Canal

Åby Fjord

Bridge Fjord

Gullmarn Fjord

Uddevalla

Havstensfjord

Malmö Fjord

Kornö

Brandskärsflak

Lysekil **9**

Fiskebäckskil

4

3

Grundsund

Gull-
holmen

Hättan

Stocken

Hälleviksstrand

Käringön

Måseskär

Mollö Sound **7**

Björholmen

6 Kyrkesund

Ellösefjord

ORUST

Slussen

Koljö Fjord

Henån

Kungsviken

Ljungskile

Svanesund

Askerön

Halsefjord

Askerö Fjord

Stenungsund

Lyre Sound

Stif Fjord

Edhultshall

TJÖRN

8 Skärhamn

Hake Fjord

Klädesholmen

Eggskär

Åstol

Dyrön

Nordön

Marstrand's Fjord

Pater Noster

Marstrand **2**

Hätteberget

Northern River

SKAGERRAK

Flag of the historical Province
of Bohuslan

SWEDISH
WEST COAST
SOUTH BOHUSLÄN

10 NAUTICAL MILES

AUSSCHNITT

Berlin

Carlsten Fortress – the last soldiers didn't leave until the early 1990s.

Two passenger ferries shuttle between the two halves of the city.

2 MARSTRAND

Mastrand's greatest attraction is visible from far out to sea: Carlsten Fortress. This unique structure on the coast was built in the 17th century to protect what was then an important trading port. Those days are long gone, but today the seaside resort attracts holidaymakers and day trippers, especially from nearby Gothenburg. No wonder, because the island of Marstrandsö, which can only be reached by ferry (and is therefore traffic-free), offers many cafés and restaurants in the historic streets as well as the view from the fortress battlements.

MOORINGS

Best in the visitor harbour on Marstrandsö (book well ahead!).

3 FRUNDSUND

Fishing used to be very important along the entire coast of Bohuslän. This is evidenced not only by the memorial stone in front of the bright white Church of the Cross and the red-painted sheds with ship names in the harbour, but also by the many captains' houses with a view of the water – even if only of the narrow (and partly artificial) canal that runs through the middle of the harbour and makes the western part (as in Marstrand) an island. A relaxed holiday resort away from the tourist crowds.

MOORINGS

For visitors on both sides of the harbour at the pier (alongside or with stern anchor, protected by the breakwater); in the Grundsunds Marina at the southern exit of the channel on request.

The canal through the middle of town.

4 FISKEBÄCKSKIL

In the north-west of the island of Skaftö, the houses of Fiskebäckskil stand on either side of a shallow bay. There is little to indicate that the place was still home to a whole fleet of cargo sailors in the 19th century. Fiskebäckskil's most famous son also came from a seafaring family: the artist Carl Wilhelmson, born in 1866, later immortalised the people and motifs of this coast in many paintings.

MOORINGS

Lyckans Slip Marina on the western shore of the bay.

5 SMÖGEN

Smögen feels like an outpost in the Skagerrak. The houses, sheds and warehouses of the small fishing village at the southern end of Hasselösund seem to be hiding from the wind and weather in the shelter of its bare granite flanks, and where herring used to be salted, malt whisky now rests to mature – with a very special aroma, of course. Other attractions include the daily fish auction and the Kleven Nature Park with its bizarrely shaped rocks.

MOORINGS

Very full in summer! Therefore, moor alongside at Smögenbryggan, further inland in the harbour with a mooring.

Smögen – a small fishing village in south Hasselösund.

6 KYRKESUND

Kyrkesund – the guest pier can be seen at the bottom left.

From the rocky heights above Kyrkesund, the outlook stretches far out over the Skagerrak. A good place to view Bohuslän's most famous seascapes is the four stone beacons known as 'St Olav's Valar'. The story goes like this: 1,000 years ago, the brothers Harald and Olav fought over the throne of Norway. A boat race was to decide the matter once and for all. While Harald chose to continue across the open sea, Olav sailed through the narrow passage where Kyrkesund now stands. In doing so, he disturbed seven trolls who knew magic and tried to stop him, but the Viking turned the trolls into stone and won the race. Four of them can still be seen today.

MOORINGS

About ten visitor berths alongside the wooden pier on the eastern shore of the sound.

Contrary to the popular image of the country, not all houses in Sweden are red or white!

The windmill at Mollösund.

7 MOLLÖSUND

Windmills are a rare sight on Sweden's west coast – especially when they also serve as a landmark for sailors. Mollösund's windmill, which has even been featured on a postage stamp, was used not only to grind grain in its heyday, but also for the production of fish food.

MOORINGS

30 visitors can moor in the harbour basin on mooring lines.

8 SKÄRHAMN

The largest harbour on the western side of the island of Tjörn is Skärhamn, which, with 4,000 inhabitants, is also the regional centre. Skärhamn cannot compete with the picture-book charm of nearby Kyrkesund, but the visitor harbour is excellently equipped, and the supply facilities are great.

Even culture is not neglected, for here you can find the Nordic Watercolour Museum, which specialises in contemporary artists from all five Scandinavian countries. An interesting concept, because the soft light of the north can really be captured with watercolours – although abstract works are displayed as well as landscape paintings.

MOORINGS

Floating jetties with stern buoys or mooring lines.

There is a boat outfitter and petrol station right by the harbour.

The guest harbour in Skärhamn is centrally located so within easy reach of everything, from the art gallery to the liquor store.

The jetties at Lyckans Slip Marina in Lysekil. There are 30 berths available for visiting boats. The exit to Gullmarfjord can be seen in the background on the right.

9 LYSEKIL

After a week of picturesque archipelago harbours, Lysekil, with its almost 8,000 inhabitants, modern housing developments, neo-Gothic stone church and freight terminal, looks almost like a big city. In addition, there is a harbour promenade and, of course, a large selection of bars, cafés and restaurants. And if it gets too much for you, you can simply take the passenger ferry across to Fiskebäckskil (No. 4)…

Text: Christian Tiedt

MOORINGS

200 berths for visitors on moorings with stern buoy and line at Havsbadets Gästhamn.

The mix of modern and traditional in the marina at Lysekil.

The view across the Sound towards the Swedish coast from the old fortress island of Trekroner.

11 SOUTH SWEDEN

Mankell's Wallander, two beautiful sisters and the eye of a needle – you're sure of a fantastic summer cruise in Scania County and on the sound.

SCANIA COUNTY

You know this Swedish province, even without knowing it. Maybe you even have a bit of Scandinavian crime fiction on board?

Rocks encrusted with brightly-coloured lichen and shallow waters are typical of the entire Swedish coast.

1 YSTAD

They have not yet erected a monument to the writer and his character: Henning Mankell and Inspector Wallander. In the 1990s, the solitary policeman investigated a dozen cases in and around Ystad – and not only made it on to Europe's bestseller lists, but also gave the entire genre of Scandinavian crime fiction an unprecedented boom.

SCHONEN
EAST COAST

10 NAUTICAL MILES

PROVINZ
SCHONEN

Åhus **6**

*ARCHIPELAGO OF
TOSTEBERGA*

Helgeån

HANÖ BAY

Kivik **5**
Königsgrab

*Stenshuvud
Nationalpark*

Simrishamn **4**

Glimmingehus
Brantevik

Skillinge **3**

Ystad
Nybro

Kåseberga **2**

Sportboothafen
Ales Stenar
Sandhammaren

1

N

Ystad has clear landmarks when approaching – two twin water towers inland and the large silos of the commercial port right on the water.

Solid piers made of stone blocks protection from wind and swell in almost all harbours in the area, including here at Simrishamn.

At the same time, he made Ystad famous beyond the borders of Sweden. If you come here today, you can follow in Wallander's footsteps, have coffee at Fridolf's in Lingsgatan or look for his blue Peugeot in front of Mariagatan 10.

Depending on where you are coming from, Ystad is often the first landfall in southern Sweden before continuing towards Hanö Bay or Stockholm. The marina, with its 70 visitor berths (on floating docks with electricity and water), is located west of the commercial and ferry harbour. Services: sanitary building, sauna, slip, crane, petrol station (super/diesel). Utilities in town – and the beach is just next door.

'Stones of Ale': 59 upright boulders form the tapering shape of a ship at the bow and stern. Probably erected around the year 600 and long covered by sand, the 'ship's setting' was restored for the first time around 100 years ago. Its purpose is still obscure. Nevertheless, it is a good place to let your thoughts wander while enjoying the wide view over the Baltic Sea.

There are about 20 alongside visitor berths in the municipal harbour, with electricity and water on the pier, plus sanitary building, slip, snack bar and kiosk. Restaurant and country store in the village (300 metres). The Ales Stenar are about ten minutes away on foot.

2 KÅSEBERGA

Just under 9 nautical miles to the east, the Ales Stenar rise up from the edge of the cliff – the

3 SKILLINGE

The first safe port of call north of Sandhammaren is Skillinge, a small fishing village with a surprisingly large harbour. The village itself can be explored quickly, but with the on-board bicycle and a little time, Glimmingehus, one of the best-preserved medieval castles in Scandinavia, is also within reach, 8 kilometres inland. Harbour services: electricity, water, slip, crane and diesel filling station.

4 SIMRISHAMN

This is a popular tourist destination, especially in summer. Not only does it have a pleasant town centre with colourful captains' houses and lots of restaurants and cafés, there's also a fine beach in the north, complete with beach bar. The centrally located marina is one of the largest in the area and offers full service in addition to 80 visitor berths on floating pontoons.

Fishing vessels can be found in every coastal town in the region. The Swedish fleet has the largest annual catch in the Baltic Sea.

5 KIVIK

At the harbour of Kivik, on the other hand, things are usually more relaxed; smoke curls into the sky from the white chimney of the fish smokehouse, and a nature reserve with a little beach and shady trees beckons along the coast. But things get lively at the end of July, when Kiviks Marknad, one of Sweden's most traditional country markets, is held over three days. However, by the time the apple festival comes around at the end of September – it's the country's largest fruit-growing area – the boating season is already over. Also worth a visit: barely a kilometre from the harbour, you can visit a 'royal tomb' from the Bronze Age, which surprises visitors with its artistic rock paintings. In Kivik, visitors are assigned one of the ten mooring places (with stern buoy).

6 ÅHUS

To reach Schonen's northernmost harbour, you have to enter the Helgeån River. Passing the container terminal on the starboard side, you will reach Åhus after 1 kilometre. Here, you can moor on the forested southern shore at Christiansstads Segelsällskap, or at the municipal jetty on the northern shore right in the town. Water, electricity and sanitary facilities are available on both sides.

What is unusual is that the town is known all over the world – without anyone knowing it. The secret is hidden within the red-brick buildings right by the pier: it was here in 1879 that Lars Olsson Smith first produced a witty drink that is still sold in distinctive pharmacy bottles today – Absolut Vodka. The distillery can be visited.

COPENHAGEN/MALMÖ

Just 14 nautical miles lie between these cities. There are differences, but also things that connect them – and that doesn't just mean the bridge over the Øresund. The end of our summer trip last year showed us both sides.

Admittedly, the comparison is not entirely fair. On the one side: Copenhagen, the glittering metropolis with millions of inhabitants, a royal capital, which with some justification is even flattered as the 'Venice of the North'. And on the other side of the Øresund: the... well, the 'city opposite'.

Most people can't think of much more to say about Malmö. This is hardly surprising, because even on Sweden's comparatively short west coast, the country's third-largest city has to compete with the second largest – and it's not easy to emerge from the long shadow of Gothenburg with its elegant and sophisticated flair.

At least the touring skippers who were on the move in the straits, belts and sound could hardly be blamed for their ignorance of Malmö – because unlike in Copenhagen, there were simply no visitor moorings near the city centre. This changed in 2010 with the completion of Dockan Marina, and according to the motto 'better late than never', the *boote* crew finally set course for this blank spot on the cruising map of our editorial office last summer. Luckily – because we were immediately impressed by Malmö. So overboard with all prejudices: from now on there are two beautiful sisters on the Øresund. All the better!

Entering the Dockan Marina in Malmö, the former dry dock of the Kockums shipyard. In the 1960s, the company was still one of the world's largest cargo shipbuilders.

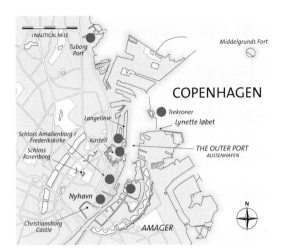

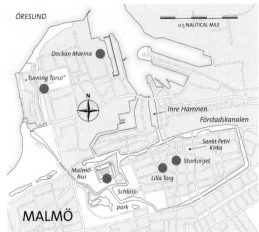

We have come from the south, taken the shortcut through the Falsterbo Canal, which saves us the diversions around the sandy peninsula with its offshore reef, and on the journey from Stralsund via Bornholm and Hanö Bay we now have the last two stages ahead of us: Malmö and Copenhagen.

The Cruising Club of Switzerland's *Rolling Swiss II* follows the narrow channel that connects to the canal in the north until we turn on to the side channel to the Øresund Bridge.

Far on the port side, a forest of offshore wind turbines stands in front of the horizon, the jets of the Copenhagen-Kastrup hover above us, and then we finally pass the bridge: 40 metres clearance, no danger for the antennas… Malmö is now already on the starboard side, overlooked by the city's new landmark, the 190-metre-high 'Turning Torso', whose gleaming white façade seems to twist into the sky. At the Flintrännan beacon we have reached the approach, which now leads to the Vågbrytarbank beacon, and then around a breakwater in front of the harbour entrance into Dockan Marina.

The long basin – as the name suggests – used to belong to the dry dock of a shipyard.

The view from Copenhagen's Inner Harbour of Amalienborg Castle Square, with the equestrian statue of King Frederik V and the Marble Church, whose 30-metre-high dome is the largest in Scandinavia.

Copenhagen's Royal Opera House on Holmen Island was open in 2005. A gift from the shipping magnate Arnold Mærsk Mc-Kinney Møller, it is now an integral part of the panorama of the Outer Harbour.

The mighty bollards on the promenade still stand and remind us of the time when riveting hammers rattled here and later welding torches hissed. But where there used to be warehouses and construction sheds, there are now rows of multi-storey residential buildings. The concept of exclusive living space on the waterfront is no longer new; London invented it in the Docklands, and it has found imitators all over the world. But here, with a largely unobstructed view of the Øresund, it has a special charm.

Visitor berths (in boxes, alongside only on the inside of the breakwater and at the inner end) are marked with green signs in the almost 350-metre-long basin, and there is a sanitary building.

Off to the city: from our mooring we walk more or less alongside the water, over the bascule bridge and the university bridge to the inner harbour and once over the suburban canal. The Stortorget, with the equestrian statue of King Karl X Gustav, is bustling with people, the town hall festively flagged. For a relaxing coffee, we continue to Lilla Torg, whose historic half-timbered houses and colourful facades give us the impression of suddenly being in a small Swedish town. Evening descends slowly, but it is warm enough and the lawns in the castle park near the massive Malmöhus are full of young people. The sounds of guitars and singing mingle with cheerful laughter. The smell of barbecue wafts into the air. A bench becomes free just in time for us to let this beautiful evening fade away a little before we return on board.

The next morning we sail 14 nautical miles across the Øresund, which lies as smooth as glass in front of us in calm conditions. Between the island of Saltholmen in the south and the former naval fortress of Flakfortet, our Trader 42 is heading for Lynetteløbet, the pleasure craft entrance to Copenhagen's inner harbour, past gleaming fuel depots and the next fortress island – but today on Trekroner, the only drill practised is local recreation.

Directly ahead, two cruise ships and the *Eclipse*, a 160-metre mega-yacht, are alongside the Langelinie – and on this summer day in the middle of Copenhagen, just about everything else that floats and has propulsion is on the water, from pedal boats to excursion steamers. Let's go for a tour of the harbour!

Still within sight of the funnels of *Queen Mary 2* and Co, the Langelinie Lystbådehavn lies across to starboard – the best 'address' if you want to be centrally located (and can find a free place). The leafy, star-shaped ramparts of the fort tower above it, and in front of it, against a colourful backdrop of coaches and

An entire city quarter has developed around the modern marina at Tuborg Havn, which is also home to the Royal Danish Yacht Club (KDY). In the past, the beer from the famous brewery was loaded here.

crowds of tourists, the Little Mermaid sits somewhat forlornly on her rock, her gaze shyly averted from dozens of cameras.

A full excursion boat ploughs ahead, waving hands through the air. By contrast, legs dangle casually from the harbour wall, faces turned towards the sun. If you are looking for shade, you are right under the overhanging roof of the opera house, now on the port side. On the other side, the restored warehouses of Toldbodgade are followed by Amaliehaven with a view past the fountain to Amalienborg Palace and the shiny dome of Frederikskirke, inspired by St Peter's Basilica in Rome. The last point of our little tour is the maritime heart of the city, the Nyhavn with its traditional ships. Those who get a berth here in the outdoor area in front of the bridge are not only blessed by luck – but probably also got up *really* early...

Four 206m-high pylons support the two-storey bridge in the 490m-wide main passage. The clearance height is 55m.

ØRESUND

The Øresund was the most important navigable deep-water route between the two seas until the inauguration of the Kiel Canal in 1895 – at that time still under the name of Kaiser Wilhelm. A fact that paid off in cash for the Kingdom of Denmark for a long time: until the middle of the 19th century, all passing ships had to pay a customs duty. The collection was made easier by the fact that the Øresund forms a real bottleneck between the Danish island of Zealand and the coast of Scania for more

than 50 nautical miles. The northern narrows at Helsingør and Helsingborg measure just 2.5 nautical miles and are still crossed by ferries in shuttle services. At the southern narrows between the small Danish town of Dragør and the Malmö suburb of Bunkeflostrand, a fixed 14-kilometre-long crossing has existed since 2000, the eastern section of which is constructed as a tunnel. On the western section, from the artificial island of Peberholm to the Swedish mainland, the Øresund Bridge spans the Baltic Sea.

Text: Christian Tiedt

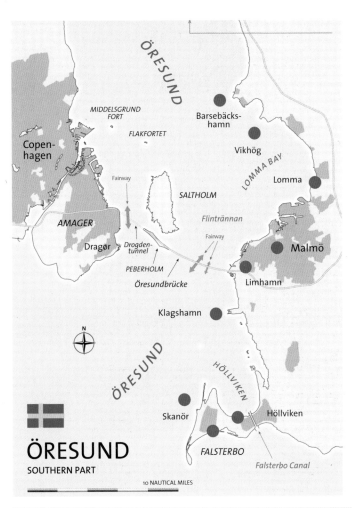

The Øresund is shallow, so larger vessels must keep the buoyed and lit channels. There are two main fairways and one side fairway.

ÖRESUND

MIDDELSGRUND FORT

FLAKFORTET

Copenhagen

Barsebäckshamn

Vikhög

LOMMA BAY

Lomma

Fairway

SALTHOLM

Flintrännan

AMAGER

Dragør

Drogden-tunnel

Fairway

Malmö

PEBERHOLM

Öresundbrücke

Limhamn

Klagshamn

N

ÖRESUND

HÖLLVIKEN

Skanör

Höllviken

FALSTERBO

Falsterbo Canal

ÖRESUND

SOUTHERN PART

10 NAUTICAL MILES

All fairways are fully lit. This is Drogden Fyr at the southern approach to Copenhagen. In the background is the wind farm of Lillgrund.

12 STOCKHOLM ARCHIPELAGO

Sailing in Napoleonsviken Bay near the island of
Ägnö in the Stockholm Archipelago.

You will certainly understand why so many sailors consider it Sweden's sailing mecca when you cruise around the Stockholm Archipelago.

Don't be alarmed: *Storm* is written in big letters on the stern of our Bavaria 40. A strange name for a charter yacht, and one from the Holiday series at that. 'Relax' or 'Sunshine' would be more appropriate. That's exactly what it looks like for the forthcoming post-season trip: sunshine and moderate wind, the best sailing conditions in the Stockholm Archipelago.

The crew, having just arrived, want to get going as quickly as possible. More or less patiently, they wait for the obligatory briefing. The most important question to be answered for the voyage, in an area with 30,000 islands and shoals: How reliable is the plotter? Can the electronics be trusted unconditionally or only to a limited extent?

Simon, the young man from the charter company Navigare Yachting, nods. Yes, yes, shoals are indicated quite accurately, he says – but in the same breath, he strongly

Heading out of Stockholm and past the fortifications on the offshore islands.

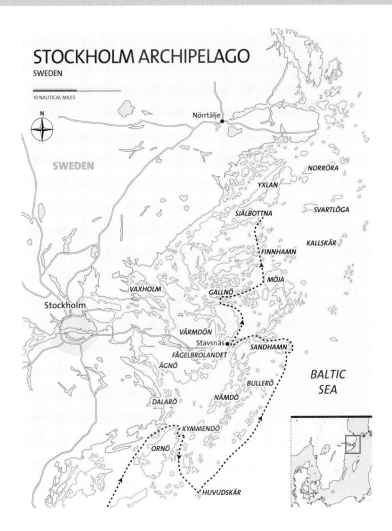

recommends always keeping an eye on the paper chart. In other words, to navigate analogue – that is, classically – at all costs. 'Just last week, another crew ran on to the rocks because they forgot to zoom in far enough on the plotter,' Simon reports.

All right, the crew nods thoughtfully, message received loud and clear: caution is the word. As soon as you leave the marked fairways, increased vigilance is required. Unlike in the Mediterranean or the tropics, here you can no longer see the shoals with the naked eye as soon as they are just a touch below the surface of the water. So it can't hurt if you have a lot of respect for the area.

It's Saturday afternoon and a nice breeze is blowing. After leaving the harbour, orientation is a bit tricky at first. The charts are small scale, and every 4 to 5 nautical miles we have to get the next sheet. There is no conventional chart, so we are forced to use the rough chart of the Waxholmsbolaget ferry connections in order not to lose sight of the big picture. We don't have anything better on board.

From this point of view, it is quite helpful that there are lots of other sailors, ferries and excursion steamers on the way at the weekend. They are like signposts to help you find fairways and passages more quickly. Without guarantee, of course. On the other hand, the

Sailing in the inner archipelago.

traffic on the water also requires increased vigilance. The genoa should suffice as a sail on day one in view of the wind force of 4 to 5. It is better to sail with the brakes on in the narrow channels. First get a feel for the area. Besides, there is a lot to see not only on the water but also on land. One crew member is reminded of the Hamptons during the first miles.

Our first destination is Vaxholm. More important than the historic fortress is the local supermarket. There is no supermarket at the charter base. So first the provisions, then culture. The strong wind blows across the boat in the narrow marina and does not make mooring manoeuvres easy. Praise be to the bow thruster, especially on our high-sided yacht.

At least as pleasing is the new crew member who, once the shopping is done,

more than makes up for his lack of sailing skills with advanced cooking skills. Very practical, like having a three-star ship's cook. Especially in Sweden, where a visit to a restaurant can make a big dent in the boat's budget.

The next day, there's 'circulating doldrums', as the sailing novice puts it. And a full-blown headache for the skipper. To a certain extent, as confirmation of the weather report that a cyclone really is approaching. A quick look at the charter base's map: the tips for one- and two-week trips in the archipelago. Finnhamn is marked with a red dot.

In the guidebook, however, the natural harbour further west called Paradiset is featured. That sounds promising!

The headsail and mainsail are quickly unfurled, and the Bavaria picks up speed quite nicely. Even a fellow sailor, who until recently was the owner of a J 97, admits that. Which is quite something!

We sail anti-cyclically, that is, against the fleet of weekend returnees. The further Stockholm stays astern, the sparser the buildings and the daintier the holiday cottages ashore. Thus, we have to share Paradise(t) – contrary to the description in the Swedish guidebook – with only one yacht. Behind a narrow entrance, there is what feels like an inland waterway with the kind of all-round protection usually only advertised by insurance companies.

At the push of a button, the stern gangway, the bathing platform, is lowered. And shortly afterwards, a man jumps from the bow pulpit on to the glacier-like shiny rocks. The rest is amazement. And rapture. The bay lives up to its name; it's hard to imagine a more beautiful place to moor a boat. It's like being in Abraham's Swedish bosom. Thanks to the low evening sun, even now, at the end of summer, a collective swim is in order. The only blemish in the paradise setting: just in time for dinner, the mosquitoes descend on the boat and the sailors as dusk falls.

By the third day at the latest, you are 'in'. As a skipper, you have developed a feeling for the area and trust in the plotter. You even dare to leave the fairways at a crawl, which sharpens your senses and increases your attention to navigation. This is absolutely necessary in

A romantic sunset in the Marina Vaxholm.

On the skerry near the
island of Idholmen.

A dilapidated hut at Gallnö.

the stony garden, which has a tendency to become a labyrinth. On the first pages of the inner archipelago, more land than water is printed on the paper. Only further out, towards the open Baltic Sea, is the ratio gradually reversed: light-blue areas, marked with two-digit water depths, and only a few archipelagos predominate there. Sometimes it looks less like a nautical chart than a star atlas.

At the beginning of September, there are hardly any other sailors to be seen in the archipelago during the week. Occasionally, a ferry passes in the distance, giving a hint of where the safe waters are. And so there is always a considerable sense of relief when, after an 'off-road' detour, we find our way back between the rows of buoys without being damaged.

We make a stopover at Norröra. Practically a compulsory visit. Astrid Lindgren's *Holidays*

on Saltkråkan was filmed here. In summer, 200 people live on the island; in winter, there are just ten. There is neither a hotel nor a café in the village. There is not even a hint that collective childminding culture was immortalised here on celluloid. Which is somewhat pleasing. There is probably also a bit of self-protection, so that the island idyll is preserved and no Disneyland offshoot is created.

In the evening we land in the marina at Furusund. It is located directly on the shipping lane leading to Stockholm. You could easily open a yacht-welcoming facility here – the traffic is as heavy as on the Elbe.

At dawn, and with the first drops of rain, we take the precaution of moving to Norrtälje. Despite a large construction site near the harbour, the small town proves to be a charming choice for being blown over and soaked. It is stormy with 7 to 8 force winds, reason enough to double the mooring line. An abandoned motor yacht has already drifted past the sauna window. And two or three other ships are suddenly lying across between the pontoons. The rescue cruiser has to come and moor them again. Real harbour cinema.

The next day the cyclone has passed; the wind has taken a Rockford turn. *Storm* sails out of the long Norrtälje Sound with an ideal port breeze and sets course for Svartlöga. That was a tip from the underworked lady at the tourist office. Only the waters around the archipelago are said to be particularly treacherous. The

Grinda Wardshus, a top destination for gourmets.

A ferry is heading for the harbour of Vaxholm under the light of a full moon.

guidebook says that due to a land uplift, the actual jetty can no longer be approached. And blocking the jetty at the back for the one ferry a day is not a good idea either. But after all, what are an anchor and a dinghy on board for!

The anchor manoeuvre and the subsequent shore leave are worth it. Fields of moss and blueberries are everywhere between rocky outcrops – 'Fifty Shades of Green' sums it up quite well. Lush flora and fauna. Swathes of dragonflies buzz above boardwalks. At the former fishermen's settlement, in the perfect picture-postcard idyll between the typical red-washed houses, we meet one of three permanent residents, Mr Schlecker. His tail-wagging dog has been following us for some time. His master looks insanely good and

healthy – a bit like Clint Eastwood. He is fetching water from the well. Since he retired, he has lived on Svartlöga all year round, even in winter. Then everything around here is frozen over and the ferry service is suspended; instead, you can go cross-country skiing or ice-skating on the Baltic Sea. He runs errands by snowmobile in winter. A dream, he says. Perfect solitude less than 60 kilometres from Stockholm as the crow flies.

Is it possible to intensify the solitude? The answer is clear: yes, you can. A little further out, on Kallskär, for example. Where the Baltic Sea attacks more frontally in winter and the growth on the rocks is correspondingly sparser. The number of red holiday cottages also decreases considerably there. Shortly

A picture postcard idyll on Norröra, also known as 'Seacrow Island'.

The north exit from Paradiset at Finnhamn.

before sunset, the natural harbour described in the guidebook unfortunately proves to be too narrow for a 12-metre yacht. The entrance looks like a garage at best. There are reeds in the apex of the bay. Who knows if the indicated water depth is still correct? That would be a hara-kiri manoeuvre, far too risky – given the fact that we are all alone out here, no other vessel for miles around.

Of necessity and in the last light of the day, which is already getting noticeably shorter, we move to a bay in the north of the archipelago. The trees are missing. And the marked eyebolts in the rocks are not there either. And the wind is howling. Fortunately, someone has put up a trustworthy mooring in front of his hut. It comes in more than handy. It's not

an appealing idea to have to keep looking for shelter here at the edge of Scania County in the dark.

The next morning, the gloom is a bit more visible: fog everywhere. A ghostly atmosphere, as if one had been driven to Greenland overnight. Stone whale humps with moss and bonsai trees on their backs. We wait for the first breeze to lift the veil and motor to Grinda, due to lack of wind, for a change of crew. Back to civilisation, which is rarely more than four or five hours away in the archipelago.

In the evening, a stylish get-together at the Grinda Wärdshus. Supposedly one of the top culinary addresses in the archipelago, and certainly not for the budget-conscious. The food is good, the atmosphere pleasantly

A small museum, housed in a hunting lodge, provides information about the flora and fauna on remote Bullerö. The island is a protected nature reserve.

relaxed. The tables are full of yachtsmen, still in their sailing gear, who come here to ring in the weekend. Others, a birthday group of dentists, have flown in by helicopter. The world is going to pot.

The next day we set off for the heart of the archipelago: Sandhamn – a kind of Mecca for sailing Swedes. The Gotland Round Regatta starts here every year. We pass two regatta panels on the way. When we arrive on the island, we decide on the Royal Swedish Sailing Club's branch on Lökholmen, opposite

One of the three permanent residents of Svartlöga.

Stockholm and its harbours are much livelier.

Sandhamn. Ideal for those who are not looking for a lively party.

In fresh northerly winds, the berth is also more sheltered. There is a free boat shuttle from the pretty harbour to Sandhamn. And a sauna. Perfect for our second harbour day, which was forced on us by the weather. But nobody complains. Why should they? The crew knows that sweating in a sauna overlooking Stockholm's Scania archipelago – probably the most beautiful suburb in the world – beats being blown away. All the best spots and bays are comparatively easy to reach here. All you have to do is navigate carefully and keep an eye on the plotter and map.

Text: Jan Jepsen

135

13 GÖTA CANAL

There is no time for boredom on the Göta Canal, with 58 locks and countless bridges to pass, but taken at an easy pace, this is a wonderful route across Sweden.

At the beginning of September, the summer begins to falter. At the latitude of the Stockholm archipelago, shorter days and falling temperatures herald the approach of autumn. One low-pressure area after another rushes in. Time to head home. There are at least 450 nautical miles to Kiel, almost 200 of them without land cover and against the prevailing wind direction. But there is an alternative: the Göta Canal promises weather-independent chugging through lovely landscapes to then sail south under the protection of Jutland. The catch: if you want to sail through the canal before 12 June or after 16 August, you have to keep to fixed times and sail in a convoy.

In summer, an army of students ensures the smooth operation of the 58 locks and countless bridges. In the so-called booking season, on the other hand, only a handful of lock keepers work, accompanying each boat convoy by car

or bicycle. Passage must therefore be booked at least five days in advance. From east to west, the journey begins on Fridays or Mondays, always at 8.30 in the morning, with check-in at the canal office in Mem. After that, the waiting yachts are sorted in groups so that they fit well into the locks.

Together with the Swedish *Soft* and the *Havneheksen* from Denmark, we are in group two. So, we can watch the first yachts being locked. Ten minutes later it's our turn. Slowly, our two companions manoeuvre into the chamber. We are lucky to be in the rear, so we get less turbulence.

The Borensberg lock staircase is the second longest in the canal. Five successive chambers raise the yachts more than 15 metres within one and a half hours.

Motala is a small town on Lake Vänern and the centre of canal administration.

On the shore there are always nicely decorated huts and houses to be seen.

After all the lines are taken, Rakel, the lock keeper, locks the gate. Silently, the gates close, slide past the flagpole by centimetres and close with a dull creak. Rakel checks once more that all crews are ready, then she opens the gates. In an instant, the chamber turns into a swirling pool and the water level begins to rise. Whoever is in front now has their work cut out for them. Winches rattle to keep the bow lines taut and the yachts close to the lock wall. About eight minutes later, the water flow stops. The upper gate opens silently and we have climbed the first 3 metres. About 31 more to go today.

Only two of the 58 locks are still operated by hand, the others can be opened and closed at the touch of a button.

Long lines are required for locking, but the manoeuvring procedure is relatively simple and quickly becomes familiar.

141

The narrow Billströmen in the approach to Lake Viken is one of the most rustic stretches of the inland waterways.

The first few kilometres of the canal are easy. Our group of three moves along at a leisurely 5 knots. On the densely wooded north bank, branches hang low into the water. To the south, the landscape is more open; the view sweeps over meadows and fields.

Then it's time to get ready for the next lock. At Tegelbruckets Sluss, a crew member has to be lowered down with the bow line for the first time. A procedure that is repeated several times over the next few hours and days and soon becomes routine. The advantage of the off-season: even if the manoeuvre is not successful at the first attempt, there is no rush. Apart from your own convoy, there is no traffic. Even the convoy itself is staggered by the locks. Over

Heading out into Lake Vänern. The Göta Canal ends in Sjötorp.

of nine chambers and a bascule bridge to be negotiated. The last four locks are so close together the crew has to walk alongside the boats.

When we reach Lake Asplågen, the auto-pilot takes over. Coffee break. After two more locks and four bridges, Norsholmen is ahead. But the railway crosses the canal beyond the bridge. Alexander, the lock keeper, had warned us: 'The bridge opening has to be cleared by the railway traffic control centre. If you're unlucky, it takes time.' We are unlucky and are stuck for more than an hour. Only then is there a green light, and the bridge folds out of the way, along with the overhead line.

The schedule has Berg on the other side of Lake Roxen as the night port. Normally, the 27-kilometre-long body of water is not a nautical challenge. But in the middle of the lake, the echo sounder starts to jump; sometimes the display shows well under 2 metres, but fortunately the dreaded tilt does not occur.

The evening approach to Berg provides further excitement. The leading light marked on the map is defective, and the fairway buoyage makes itself scarce. Instead, the echo sounder permanently reports shallow water. With the help of the plotter image, the approach nevertheless succeeds, *Havneheksen* and *Soft* following in our wake.

Shortly before 9pm, the lines are tight. The result of the day: 15 locks, 31 metres of altitude, ten bridges. Outside on the lake, the position lanterns of the last lock group are visible. In complete darkness, they have less luck with the approach. Shortly before the harbour, the two yachts suddenly change

long stretches, only the three or four boats of each lock group travel together. In addition, the lock occupancy remains the same, so it is always clear which yachts are in the chamber.

Nevertheless, there is hardly any time to catch one's breath. On the first stretch in particular, the manoeuvres take place every ten minutes. There are seven locks with a total course, then stop. They are obviously looking for the fairway.

Shortly afterwards, the *Nadir* crew arrives. Anita and Kai are less lucky with the *Sea-Maid*. They get stuck in the entrance and have to be towed in by dinghy. The next morning the problem becomes clear: the lake is extremely weedy. As soon as you leave the channel mowed by the canal steamers, you run the risk of getting stuck in the underwater undergrowth.

Day two begins with the Carl-Johan lock stairs at Berg. In seven successive chambers, the ascent is just under 19 metres. This procedure, which is now routine, takes about two hours. This is followed by two more double sluices with another 10 metres of lift. Even in the off-season, busloads of tourists scurry across the impressive facility – usually at the point about to be occupied by a mooring line.

After the lock system lies astern, the waterway winds past sparse oak forests through an open agricultural landscape. The canal level is slightly elevated, which guarantees a good view. In front of the picturesque backdrop of the Göta Hotel in Borensberg lies one of the canal's last hand-operated locks. This means that the day's destination is almost reached, and there is a rare opportunity for a shore leave. An old stone arched bridge leads into the small town. Apart from a few restaurants, Borensberg offers one of the few opportunities to stock up on fresh provisions in the off-season. You should take advantage of this opportunity, because most of the cafés and shops along the quay are closed.

Whereas the water so far has been mostly greenish-brown, the Boren is clearer. But here, too, the water plants are sprouting, so you are well advised to stick to the route of the canal

steamers. The night harbour at Borenshult is not very inviting. The sanitary facilities consist of a basic toilet, and the shore has been taken over by geese and their droppings.

The next morning, it's a 15-metre climb up the canal's second-longest lock staircase. Past the historic Motala Verkstad, we head into the town of Motala – and on to Vättern. The bright yellow Götakanalbolaget, the seat of the canal administration, is enthroned directly on the lakeshore. On Sundays in the off-season, the pretty town doesn't have much to offer. A cup of coffee at the market and the lunch buffet in the old harbour warehouse are part of a short tour.

There, all the crews of the small convoy family meet again before parting ways. Only the crews of *Soft* and *Havneheksen* want to sail the entire channel. The other yachts will go into winter storage on Vättern.

On the lake, sailing could finally begin again. But the wind is whispering at 4 knots, and the road bridge in Karlsborg has to be passed at 6pm on the dot. So the engine stays on. The 'land in sight' is waiting in front of the bridge. We had already met Anke and Matthias in Finland. They left their convoy and spent a few days on the lake. Now they join our group. Such convoy changes should be announced when booking the passage.

The night port will be the idyllic Forsvik, situated between two lakes. The historic industrial facilities, including the old factory railway, are now a museum and a visit is highly recommended.

Day four starts with the most untouched leg of the trip. Through passages blasted into the rock, barely 12 metres wide, the canal leads into Lake Viken, whose densely forested shores and islets are reminiscent of

The 185-year-old structure is open from 3rd May to 29th September.

northern Sweden. In Tåtorp, the canal has to be navigated by hand again. From now on, it's downhill, with the Viken the highest point at just under 92 metres above sea level.

A few bridges later, the canal winds through meadows and fields again. By 4pm, the day's destination, Töreboda, is already ahead. The early stop gives us time to take advantage of the well-stocked supermarket. Diesel is stored in canisters at the nearby petrol station, as the boat refuelling stations, like many others in the area, are already in hibernation.

The last leg leads to Sjötorp on Lake Vänern the next morning. This marks the end of the Göta Canal and the convoy trip, and a little melancholy sets in. During the past five days, our little group has become a community. Telephone numbers and email addresses are exchanged. The remaining route over Lake Vänern and through the Trollhättan Canal to Gothenburg can be travelled all year round without time pressure. This makes individual cruise planning possible again.

Text: Hauke Schmidt

14 FINLAND

The new marina on the former fortress island of Örö.

Taking in the Finnish archipelago and with a detour to Tallinn in Estonia, a trip to this part of the Baltic Sea will show you its own special charm.

Secretly, the fog has laid an ambush. Just a moment ago it seemed content to remain on the open sea, a harmless strip on the horizon, against which the silhouettes of the sunlit archipelago stood out clearly. But now, suddenly, at the narrowest point of the fairway, with a flat rocky coast on both sides, it strikes: its white wall rolls in from the west, as if responding to a signal, and far faster than the feeble wind would suggest.

It overwhelms the island of Furuholmen, about a cable-length off starboard, and before we have time to switch on the navigation lights, it swallows us too. Visibility is no more than three boat lengths, and we hastily slow down. Surreal sunlight still glitters on the water, but other than that we are gliding through a world of grey shadows. Now we are glad we have the plotter, radar and AIS, because the sparse sea marks have become just as invisible as the

The sailing season is short, lasting from the end of June until the end of August, so harbours (such as here in Nagu) are often busy.

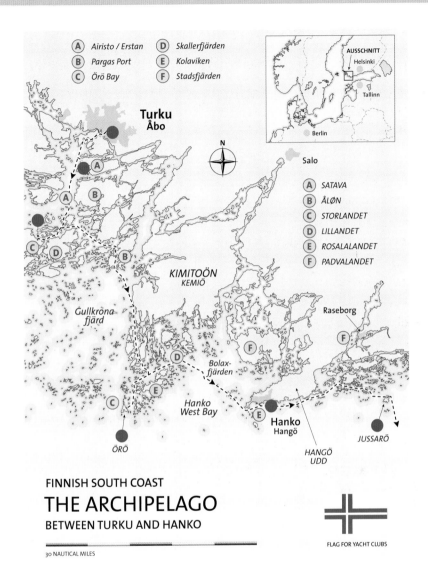

FINNISH SOUTH COAST

THE ARCHIPELAGO
BETWEEN TURKU AND HANKO

FLAG FOR YACHT CLUBS

30 NAUTICAL MILES

nearby land and the sailor ahead. Cautiously we feel our way forward.

But perhaps our destination, whose northern edge must be to starboard ahead, doesn't want to be found at all? It would be fitting – after all, the island of Örö 'existed' only in secret for a century.

The almost 4-kilometre-long skerry, strategically located at the junction of the Åland Sea and the Gulf of Finland, was a restricted military area until a few years ago. It only reopened to the public in 2015. A jetty has even been laid out for visitors on their own boat. The directional beacons for the approach (not yet marked on our current nautical chart) also date from this time. But because the island was isolated for so long, nature was able to flourish undisturbed: a small paradise that we also only found out about by chance, and a real insider tip – for now.

Just three days before, at the start of the trip in Turku in southern Finland, none of us on board had ever heard of Örö. But after taking over the *Rolling Swiss II* from our predecessors,

Most beacons are painted white and correspond in shape to the Scandinavian type.

our small crew was initially faced with a completely different challenge than the exact planning of the stages.

The rough schedule was clear enough: in the next two weeks we wanted to sail from Turku along the Finnish archipelago on an easterly course. A detour to Tallinn in Estonia should be included. The final destination was Helsinki.

However, since the cruising-club-owned Trader 42 had run aground on the last leg to Turku, our first stage took us straight to the shipyard. Fortunately, help was at hand: at reduced speed, we sailed from Turku's visitor pier on the Aurajoki River to the coast and then a few pleasant nautical miles in the

The harbour of Nagu with the 'pizza ship' at the back right of the jetty.

A calm atmosphere in Samppa on Satava.

smooth wake of a large Swedish ferry to the offshore island of Satava. Soon, the *Rolling* hung dripping in the crane straps of the marina of Satavan Venepalvelu and presented her underside: both propellers had proper dents and had to be repaired. This was done in record time, however, so that the heavy screws were shining like new on the shafts the very next day. Now, finally, the cruise could really begin.

We leave Satava early the next morning. With no wind at all, the Airisto lies before us like a mirror. The wide inlet, flanked on both sides by larger islands, leads south-west. On the wooded shore, pretty cottages – called mökki – duck in and out of the sparse greenery, complete with sauna, jetty and bathing children. A Finnish-Swedish summer idyll, because many of the people living here are Finnish-Swedes who have retained their language. Consequently, the maps are peppered with pairs of names: Turku and Åbo, Hanko and Hangö. In Finnish, the Archipelago Sea is called Saaristomeri, in Swedish Skärgårdshavet.

Our first destination of the day is called Nauvo by the Finns and Nagu by the Swedes. To reach it, we leave the deep main water at a right angle to the Skog Holm lighthouse and follow a 2.4-metre channel on the map into the labyrinth of the archipelago.

White and black cardinal signs, large floating poles made of plastic, mark the visible rocks and those hidden under water, and so

A windless evening on Jussarö.

A relaxed holiday atmosphere on the terrace in front of the harbour café on Örö.

At the boat refuelling station in Hanko.

we pass between the islands of Haverö, Kaldö and Lillandet to Storlandet, at whose north-eastern tip Nagu lies well protected in a bay.

For boaters and other trippers, the cosy little village with its almost 1,500 inhabitants is one of the most popular destinations in the area. The anchor on the coat of arms says it all. The reason for this (besides the central location and the sandy beach, which is rare here) has long been the Najaden, a former archipelago steamer that has been converted into a restaurant-bar and is better known along the coast as 'the pizza ship'. From our berth it is only a few metres across the jetty to the Najaden. While live guitar music is being played downstairs, we enjoy the white midsummer night of our first day on the sun deck with 'Pizza Inferno' (with homemade

Endless blues on the rocky coast of Jussarö.

chilli sauce) and ice-cold draught beer from Lapin Kulta.

Off to Örö! We get the tip in the harbour office of Nagu when we ask for a beautiful stopover on the way to Hanko: 'The jetty on the island has only been there since last year. It's very beautiful there!' The course of the fairway and the still new buoyage on the last part of the approach are quickly drawn on our nautical chart with a firm line.

The general course is south-east: in a slight slalom, our course line waves around one cardinal buoy after another; leading light lines – marked by staggered pairs of red-painted panels with vertical yellow bars – come into view ahead and disappear again in the wake. It gets narrow once more between the larger islands of Sorpo and Järmo, where there is also

a larger visitor harbour at the narrow passage of Pargas Port.

After that, the view opens up to the wide, sparkling waters of Gullkronafjärd, interspersed with small and tiny skerries that often have little more than a few crooked pines, a steel beacon or one of the old kummel, white-painted stone markers that used to serve for orientation and easy navigation. The southern part of the archipelago, towards which the *Rolling Swiss II* is now pointing its bow, has been designated a national park. There are 2,000 islands of all sizes in an area of 500 square kilometres, with another 8,000 in the immediate vicinity.

Sea eagles and ringed seals are as much at home here as crab apple and bloody cranesbill. A magnificent natural formation of granite and gneiss, planed smooth by the glaciers of the

The bell tower of the church of Nagu.

ice age and washed by Baltic Sea waves. The land is still rising slowly, freed from its million-ton weight, and the rocks grow out of the sea by several millimetres a year. Finally, shadowy contours emerge ahead in the fog – and masts! So, we are exactly where the plotter says we should be: in front of the island harbour of Örö. When we lay the lines over the cleats at the end of the long floating jetty, the sun is already beating down innocently from the blue sky.

The harbour office is located a little above on the rocks, which are also used as a terrace by the small island café. There is a holiday atmosphere in the air: the tempting smell of barbecue rises from the open-air steak bar,

glasses clink, and many a bikini-clad sailor worships the sun.

Soldiers stationed here will not have been quite so relaxed, but between boot polishing and weapons training they must surely have enjoyed leisure time. The first were the Russian artillerymen sent by Nicholas II to Örö in 1915 (at that time Finland was still part of the tsarist empire as a grand duchy) to protect St Petersburg from the fleet of his imperial cousin Kaiser Wilhelm II. For this purpose, he had barracks and casemates built, and installed super-heavy 305mm, 52-calibre Obukhov cannons, which could fire their shells 30 kilometres away. Örö had become a fortress.

Even today, the guns still stretch their long steel snouts out to sea, seemingly ready for action, but in fact only as camouflaged museum pieces, because the Finnish army, which continued to operate the batteries as part of the coastal defence, withdrew in 2014. Nature has taken over again, as if the military had only ever been tolerated anyway.

There won't be another fog surprise – at least not the next day: force 5 winds from the west drive whitecaps on the now deep-blue sea, and the horizon is clear. On the open Bolaxfjärden it is much rougher than in the shelter of the archipelago water off the coast of Rosalalandet. Fortunately, we don't have to head in that direction! While boats on the opposite course tumble from one wave crest to

A curious deer in the forest of Örö. The island is part of the national park.

The wild beach of Örös.

A windless evening on Jussarö.

the next and disappear repeatedly in showers of spray, we navigate dryly to the south-east, in the direction of Hanko.

We find our berth at the floating jetties of the comfortable marina of Itämeren Portti. We take the ferry across to the harbour, around which the functional centre of the likewise bilingual town of 8,000 inhabitants spreads out. The landmark of the town is the red three-legged water tower behind the church, which

you can climb. In the evening we sit down on board to plan the rest of the cruise. Before we cross the Gulf of Finland for our detour to Tallinn, we look for a starting point further east.

We choose the small island of Jussarö on the outer edge of the Ekenäs archipelago, which we reach the next day in much calmer weather after a two-hour trip. Here we are even more immersed in nature than on Örö, but there are still traces of civilisation to discover: in the middle of the dense deciduous forest that covers most of the 150-hectare island, Finland's only 'ghost town' ekes out an existence – crumbling apartment blocks with empty window cavities, sheds full of ferns and bungalows in which young birch trees grow.

In the small Café Ön right next to the harbour, which is only open during the season, we learn the history of the abandoned buildings: they belong to an iron ore mine from the 1960s. The mine still stands, too, near the isolated, grey sandy beach on the south shore. The ore reserves were not stored under the island: although the mine was drilled 250 metres deep, the shafts were driven under the

A votive ship in the church of Nagu. Until 1917 the Finns were subjects of the tsar in St Petersburg.

The water tower and church of Hanko.

163

Sailing in the archipelago south of Turku.

View southeast from Örö. Beyond the inner archipelago you can see the lighthouse of Bengtskär, the highest in the Nordic countries.

sea. The length of the underground railway was 3.5 kilometres at last count. But after six years, operation was discontinued in 1967 – due to a lack of economic efficiency.

We slowly follow the half-buried wooden skeleton of the conveyor belt back to the harbour in the north. Children are playing on the still warm rocks, Finns on a traditional sailing boat are singing folk songs, and an elderly woman is immortalising the atmosphere of this bright summer evening in watercolours on an easel. How alive even an uninhabited island can be!

Text: Christian Tiedt

Finnish icebreakers and recreational boats on the Katajanokka peninsula in the centre of Helsinki.

15 HELSINKI AND TALLINN

The season here can be quite short, lasting from the end of June until the end of August, so harbours such as Nagu can get quite crowded, but there's a good reason why these waters are so popular with sailors.

The white letters on the icebreaker's sturdy side are metres high. It says *Sisu*. The term describes a character trait that is part of the Finns' self-image and for which no single English word would suffice as a translation. For *sisu* combines toughness and tenacious endurance with elemental strength. The

perfect name for such a ship, especially as it is one of the strongest in the world.

In winter, when the sea ice makes its way to the ends of the Baltic Sea and the Bothnian Sea and the flat archipelago coasts of Finland are transformed into a frozen world, *Sisu* and its ilk are the only navigational enablers. But now, in

Tallinn's Old City Marina.

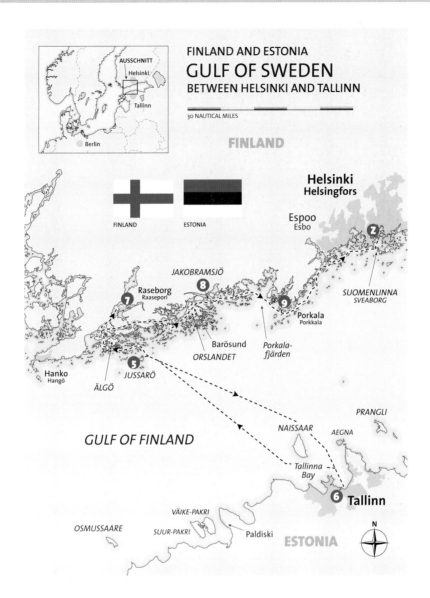

FINLAND AND ESTONIA
GULF OF SWEDEN
BETWEEN HELSINKI AND TALLINN

30 NAUTICAL MILES

FINLAND

FINLAND   ESTONIA

Helsinki
Helsingfors

Espoo
Esbo

Z

JAKOBRAMSJÖ

8

Raseborg
Raasepori

7

SUOMENLINNA
SVEABORG

9

Porkala
Porkkala

Barösund
ORSLANDET

Porkala-
fjärden

5

Hanko
Hangö

JUSSARÖ

ÄLGÖ

PRANGLI

NAISSAAR   AEGNA

GULF OF FINLAND

Tallinna
Bay

6 Tallinn

VÄIKE-PAKRI

N

OSMUSSAARE   SUUR-PAKRI   Paldiski

ESTONIA

midsummer, they slumber on heavy hawsers at the pier of the Katajanokka peninsula, right in the centre of their home port of Helsinki.

At slow speed, the *Rolling Swiss II* rounds the wide sweeping sterns of the four giants. Fortunately, the summer is far from over for us too, but there is still a feeling of farewell on board: our two-week trip, which began in Turku, will soon come to an end in the Finnish capital. The second half of our trip, the fascinating landscape of the Gulf of Finland,

lies ahead of us – and it began as it is now ending: with the approach to a Baltic Sea metropolis.

For the last six days, the destination has been Tallinn. The weather plays along: the lively north-westerly, which has accompanied us since at least Hanko but hardly troubled us in the shelter of the archipelago, takes a break at the right time. Only force 2 is forecast today. With a running sea and slightly overcast skies, we can enjoy the best conditions for the 40

One of the many ferries on the route between Tallinn and Helsinki.

nautical miles that still separate us from the Estonian capital on an ESE course.

We started in the morning on Jussarö, a rocky outpost of the Ekenäs archipelago. The winding tower of the disused iron ore mine, a block in the dense forest of the small island, slowly disappeared in our wake. Instead, the open waters of the Gulf of Finland and an empty horizon spread out before the bow of our Trader 42. The yacht belongs to the Cruising Club of Switzerland and spends most of this season with changing crews in the Baltic Sea. The Finns call the easternmost branch of the Baltic Sea, which we cross with a foaming bow wave, Suomenlahti – Bay (or Gulf) of Finland – on its northern shore, a name that has been adopted by the other littoral states, in their languages. To the south lies the small Republic of Estonia, to the east Russia with its city of St Petersburg.

After about three hours of dead-straight sailing, during which we have only met one ship, a freighter under the Russian flag, heavily marked by rust and with an oily smoke trail, the low, sandy line of the island of Naissaar comes into view to starboard ahead. We round its northern tip with the prominent lighthouse and enter the wide bay of Tallinn behind a large car ferry painted bright green. Now we can steer by sight again, because the city silhouette with its needle spires and medieval battlements (and the two equally high cruise ships in front of it) is now straight ahead over the fluttering club standard on the bow and makes any further landmark superfluous.

The floating pontoons of the Old City

The pretty guest harbour of Raseborg with its wooden pier.

Marina are located inside the city harbour. Since the outer area belongs to the ferries and is called at by several lines, the high heads of the concrete pier may only be passed after permission has been obtained by radio. This comes from 'Port Control' via channel 14, and when the traffic lights are green, we pass between ro-ro ships loading and unloading from Helsinki, Mariehamn and St Petersburg until the rectangular basin of the marina opens up in front of us. The industrial charm of the high-fenced harbour is not obvious, but we are in international company (a large merchant vessel from Portsmouth provides a certain exoticism) – and in the immediate vicinity of Tallinn's old town.

Tallinn is magnificent. This opinion is shared by the hordes of tourists who flood the historic city centre even on indifferent summer days and who ensure that there is something to buy on every corner, from fake fur hats to real amber – and everything in between. On the upside, this colourful confusion creates an almost medieval impression: this is especially true on Raekoja plats in the shadow of the Gothic town hall with its whimsical gargoyles and the watchful figure of Vana Toomas on the tallest spire. The copper soldier is one of the oldest surviving weathervanes in Europe and one of Tallinn's landmarks.

Below, where it smells of beer and spit-roasting, brave fire-eaters and modern jesters perform their art, and the great clamour of voices is only eclipsed by the rapturous chanting of saffron-robed Hare Krishna devotees, who parade around the cobbled square with drumbeats like the Anabaptists through the minster of 1530.

The only historical anomaly is caused by the entirely modern stiletto heels of the numerous Russian visitors. But away from the tourist pilgrims' paths, it soon becomes quiet, even in the alleys of the splendidly restored Vanalinn, as the old town is called in Estonian, a language that is very similar to Finnish. Relaxed cafés and small creative restaurants can be found here, as well as interesting historical insights.

For an aerial view, the path leads up through the city wall to Toompea, or Cathedral Hill. There you will find not only St Mary's cathedral church ('Dome Church')

and the Russian Orthodox Alexander Nevsky Cathedral, but also the seat of the Estonian parliament. And from a terrace hidden under trees, the Kohtuotsa, you have a clear view of the sea of red rooftops of the old town all the way to the harbour and Tallinn Bay beyond.

There is so much to see that we allow ourselves a day in the harbour. Afterwards, we had originally planned to spend another night on Naissaar, which was a restricted military area for decades, but has become a kind of festival hotspot in the capital. But now the weather is throwing a spanner in the works: the wind is supposed to pick up again considerably.

We'd rather not take any risks and we start crossing the Gulf of Finland again while it's still reasonably calm – right away.

In the afternoon it turns out that the decision was exactly right, because we have passed the first offshore archipelago and the flat Finnish coast comes into view just as the

The closer you get to the shelter of the mainland, the greener the rocky coast becomes.

The calm before the storm in the Ekenäs archipelago.

173

The heart of Tallinn's old town is Raekoja plats, with a Gothic town hall dating from 1404.

The defence tower in Tallinn houses the maritime museum.

first bad storm is brewing. In the face of the wall of black cloud, the anemometer begins to dance nervously. We pass Jussarö again ahead of a doomsday sky in the east and sail on a 5-metre side channel between large and small rocks from one sea mark to the next. Back on the main fairway, we turn to the north-east – but the bad weather has moved away and we are lucky. Golden sunlight shines as a wide, peaceful expanse of water opens up before us after the narrows at Odensö. Framed by dense forest, the Pojovik stretches deep into the land here – an arm of the sea that seems like a lake. A completely different world compared to the rough archipelago coast 'outside'.

We head for the 'oak peninsula', Ekenäs, which is almost completely surrounded by water. The village, which itself belongs to the

The view from Tallinn Cathedral Hill over the rooftops of the Old Town. On the left are the ferry port and marina.

town of Raseborg (Finnish: Raasepori, but the vast majority of the inhabitants are Finnish-Swiss), takes its name from the oak trees, which are otherwise rather rare here and can thrive sheltered from the sea.

It is a cosy place with an old pier and a real sandy beach as well as good shopping facilities. You can also wander through the historic quarter of Barkensudde, which consists almost entirely of old wooden houses and is one of the largest preserved of its kind in the Baltic region (which is not lacking in wooden houses).

The next day is dominated by gloomy grey as we follow the archipelago fairway close under land eastwards towards Helsinki. The islands are large; each bay has its own holiday home. Accordingly, there are many boats on the water, sailors under engine as well as the fast aluminium bow riders that are so typical of the area because they are often the only means of transport due to the lack of road connections.

Skärlandet passes to starboard, as well as Torsö, before we pass the narrow Barösund (with ferry and good visitor moorings) between Orslandet and Barölandet. We do not get to see the open Baltic Sea any more, as just a few nautical miles later we approach the small Jakob Ramsö, which the harbour guide describes as a quiet, natural experience: a small floating jetty in the reed-lined bay of

The museum submarine *Vesikko* on the fortress island of Suomenlinna.

Moored at Jakob Ramsjö.

Porkkala guest harbour.

the island that is shielded to the west, a café beneath a red-yellow directional beacon, and forest – that's it.

The tranquility is unquestionable, but the experience of nature is not so easy: the thicket behind the café resembles a jungle. But those who manage to follow the almost overgrown trail are at least not alone: they are soon accompanied by a whole host of happy mosquitoes.

The next day, however, we are luckier: the sky looks friendly again, and after a long beat across the open Porkalafjärden (and the narrowest rock passage of the entire archipelago – only a few metres remain on either side), we spend our last night in the archipelago at the jetty of Porkala Marin, in a sheltered bay at the outer end of the peninsula

of the same name. The small harbour with its terrace café, pizza parlour (during the day) and family restaurant (in the evening) is a regular destination for boaters and holidaymakers from the surrounding area and immediately creates a festive atmosphere. It's a great way to end the day before heading back to the big city.

Fom Porkala we head north-east towards Helsinki; the Finnish capital with its suburbs and outskirts is not far away, and it is correspondingly lively on the water as holiday and residential areas merge into one another. The city of Espoo is on the port side; apartment blocks and office buildings alternate. Now we see the ferries again, some of which we already know from Tallinn. Their terminals are in Länsisatama, the western harbour. We

The navigational beacon on the southern headland of Jakob Ramsjö, with the open sea of the Gulf of Finland beyond.

cross their fairway and make a last stopover on the former garrison and fortress island of Suomenlinna (Swiss: Sveaborg), which used to guard the waterways to Helsinki with heavy weapons and is one of its tourist attractions. We only stay two hours, but an overnight stay would have been well worth it, as there is a lot to discover, from the island museum to the preserved homes of the tsarist officers to the submarine museum *Vesikko*.

But of course, the same applies to Helsinki.

From Suomenlinna you can even see it already: the southern harbour with the excursion boats, the multi-towered Eastern Orthodox Uspenski Cathedral, the proud dome of the cathedral church and the Katajanokka peninsula, where our reserved place in the Helsinki Marina is waiting for us – and where the big icebreakers take their summer break.

Text: Christian Tiedt

Helsinki Cathedral.

A mega yacht visits the capital.

16 POMERANIAN COAST

Between Usedom and Gdansk on the Pomeranian coast lie endless beaches and other destinations worth visiting, especially for culture lovers.

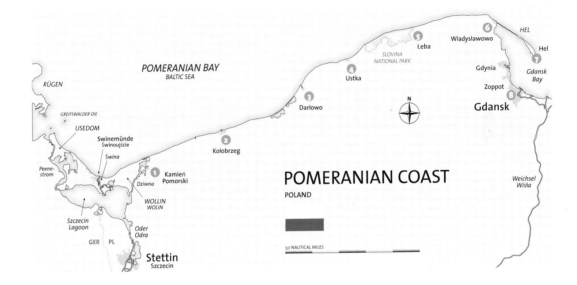

POMERANIAN BAY
BALTIC SEA

RÜGEN

GREIFSWALDER OIE

USEDOM

Swinemünde
Świnoujście

Świna

Peene-
strom

Dziwna

Kamień
Pomorski

WOLLIN
WOLIN

Szczecin
Lagoon

Oder
Odra

GER   PL

Stettin
Szczecin

Kołobrzeg

Darłowo

Ustka

SLOVINA
NATIONAL PARK

Łeba

Władysławowo

HEL

Hel

Gdynia

Zoppot

Gdansk
Bay

Gdansk

Weichsel
Wisła

N

POMERANIAN COAST

POLAND

50 NAUTICAL MILES

To the horizon: whether in the fine sand of its endless beaches or the shade of its pine forests, Poland's north offers a pure Baltic Sea feeling.

Władysławowo is a busy fishing port. Expect swells at any time of the day or night.

1 ŚWINOUJŚCIE

The westernmost of the Polish Baltic ports – Świnoujście, formerly Swinemünde – can be reached on foot from the neighbouring seaside resort of Ahlbeck: a cross-border promenade connects the German and Polish sides of the holiday island of Usedom at this point. The best visitor berths are at the modern Port Jachtowy, the marina on the west bank of the Świna (English: [river] mouth), the middle of the three connections between the Szczecin Lagoon and the open Baltic Sea. Surrounded by green spaces, the marina has floating pontoons and is located about 500 metres from the town centre, with good supply facilities.

Above: The spacious jetty at Kamień Pomorski Marina with an unobstructed view of the Cammin Bodden in the background.

Above right: Latarnia Morska Kołobrzeg – the 26-metre high lighthouse from 1948 attracts not only ships, but also tourists.

Right: The two floating pontoons of the marina at Darłowo are located in the eastern part of the harbour basin.

2 KAMIEŃ POMORSKI

About 35 kilometres further east, the marina Kamień Pomorski, which is also still quite new, awaits visitors. The modern swimming pier on the northern edge of the town is located on the eastern shore of the Cammin Bodden between the island of Wolin and the mainland. The open Baltic Sea is also only a few nautical miles away here: the way there leads across the Dziwna (Dievenow), the eastern exit of the lagoon.

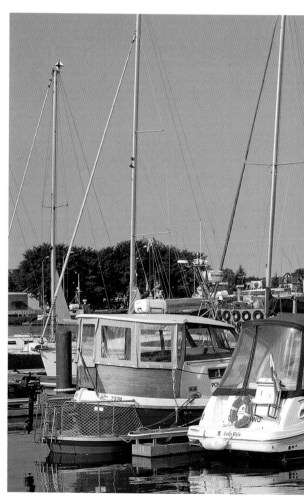

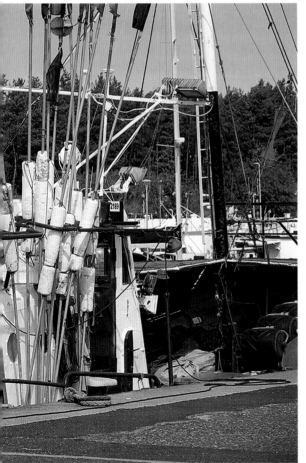

Above: Perfect for a holiday cruise in summer, you are never far from a sandy beach in Łeba.

Above left: The view from the Kołobrzeg lighthouse over the beach and the mouth of the Parsęta River, enclosed by piers. The harbour lies inland.

Left: The port of Ustka (Stolpmünde) is one of the smallest along the coast.

3 KOŁOBRZEG

For centuries, the medieval Brick Gothic cathedral has been the landmark of Kołobrzeg (formerly Kolberg). After the Second World War, a brick lighthouse was added to the harbour entrance, whose curved piers reach out into the Baltic Sea. For now, the town lives more from tourism than from fishing. The numerous new spa hotels behind the pine belt of the health resort gardens are testimony to this development. Visitor berths are available at Marina Solna (with floating pontoons and a modern service building).

4 DARŁOWO

In Darłowo, formerly Rügenwalde in German, pleasure boats and fishing vessels share the only harbour basin. After passing the pier heads, its entrance is about half a nautical mile upstream on the port side. Two 70-metre floating jetties are available there. However, it's about 2 kilometres along the banks of the Wieprza to the pleasant centre of the 14,000-inhabitant town with its old market (and supply facilities).

5 USTKA

Another seaside resort with a relaxed atmosphere along the endless sandy coast of Pomerania is Ustka, the former Stolpmünde. Here, too, you can moor centrally just a few hundred metres upstream from the pier heads, but alongside the harbour wall.

6 ŁEBA

Huge shifting sand dunes, quiet moors and floodplains: the Slovincian National Park west of the town of Łeba gives an impression of what the southern Baltic coast looked like in earlier times. The modern marina (four 70-metre floating pontoons, service building) is a good starting point for exploring the area by bus or bicycle.

The heart of Gdansk, with boats on the Motlawa.

Łeba is a favourite destination of Polish skippers, not least because of the nearby national park.

7 WŁADYSŁAWOWO

Poland's largest fishing port is located behind high concrete breakwaters and is characterised by a rather rugged charm. Tourism is now another source of income, thanks to the sandy beaches and the nearby seaside resorts.

8 HEL

In the past, Hel (formerly Hela) may have been a sleepy fishing village; today, this village at the eastern end of the peninsula of the same name – a spit about 34 kilometres long – is firmly in the hands of holidaymakers. Visitor berths are available at the floating jetty in the modern marina between the outer and middle piers.

8 GDANSK

The old Hanseatic city in the south of the Bay of Gdansk is the easternmost port of call for boats on the open Polish Baltic coast. A rich history and famous monuments such as the Crane Gate, City Hall and St Mary's Church make the Baltic metropolis a highlight in the region, as do the cultural programme and colourful nightlife. The perfect starting point for this is a place at the floating pier of the Gdansk Marina within sight of the Old Town.

Text: Christian Tiedt
Photos: Morten Strauch

The Peene River is considered the Amazon of the North – the landscape here is so pristine. The highlight at the end is the protected backwater.

The last stretch is so steep that we have to dismount: we push our suddenly unruly bikes with skidding wheels up the narrow forest path over roots, leaves and stones, while above us the sun shines through the shady canopy. But the goal is in sight: we take the last step with momentum and stand on the summit of the Streckelsberg – the highest point along the coast of Usedom.

We are rewarded with a fantastic panorama: below us the sandy cliff, whose edge drops almost 60 metres to the beach, and behind it the deep blue Baltic Sea as far as the eye can see. White sails can be seen, jet skis chasing, a cruise ship far out; even the island of Greifswalder Oie with its lighthouse stands clear as a silhouette on the horizon.

For us, this moment at lofty heights (before descending again and finally plunging into the surf at the pier in Koserow) is in a way also the highlight of our trip. This is exactly what we had planned when we set off with our charter

There is no other river valley as natural as the Peene in the whole of northern Germany. You won't find a trace of the urban world for many kilometres, such as in this densely forested part between Lake Kummerow and Demmin.

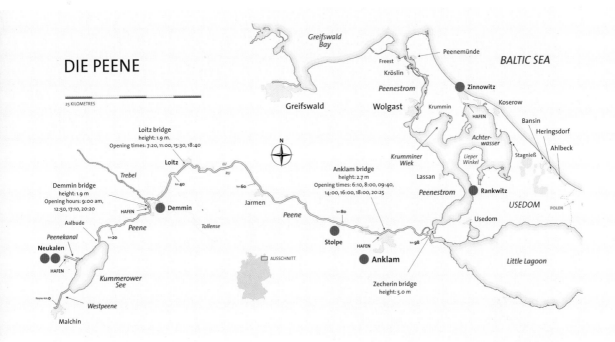

DIE PEENE

25 KILOMETRES

Greifswald
Bay

BALTIC SEA

Peenemünde

Freest

Kröslin

Zinnowitz

Peenestrom

Koserow

Greifswald

Wolgast

Krummin

HAFEN

Bansin

Heringsdorf

Loitz bridge
height: 1.9 m.
Opening times: 7:20, 11:00, 15:30, 18:40

Achter-
wasser

Ahlbeck

Loitz

EU

Krumminer
Wiek

Lieper
Winkel

Stagnieß

Trebel

EU

Anklam bridge
height: 2.7 m
Opening times: 6:10, 8:00, 09:40,
14:00, 16:00, 18:00, 20:25

Lassan

km 40

km 60

Demmin bridge
height: 1.9 m
Opening hours: 9:00 am,
12:50, 17:10, 20:20

Peenestrom

Rankwitz

Jarmen

Demmin

USEDOM

POLEN

HAFEN

Peene

Peene

Aalbude

Tollense

Usedom

Peenekanal

km 20

Neukalen

Stolpe

HAFEN

km 98

HAFEN

AUSSCHNITT

Anklam

Little Lagoon

Kummerower
See

Zecherin bridge
height: 5.0 m

Peene-km 0

Westpeene

Malchin

yacht far inland a few days ago: we were to sail on the Peene via the Peenestrom and the Achterwasser to Usedom – from the reed edge to the sandy beach!

On Friday afternoon, we arrive at the small harbour of Neukalen. Under sunshades, excursionists treat themselves to the first refreshment of the day at the Gasthaus Am Hafen, and locals are busily preparing for another weekend on the water at the colourful boathouses. In between, a handful of charter yachts stern to the jetty await their new crews. The boats – all steel displacement boats – belong to the fleet of Yachtcharter Schulz. The company from Waren operates one of its six bases here and offers inland cruises in the Peene region as well as more extensive one-way trips.

Our *Lotte*, a 12-metre steel yacht of the Schulz 40 type, is quickly spotted thanks to her sky-blue hull. The handover is also quick,

The Pomeranian griffin is an imposing addition to the fountain in the market at Anklam.

The tower of St Bartholomaei in Demmin is visible from afar.

so that we can stock up on supplies straight away. Two supermarkets (Netto and Edeka) are only a few minutes away by car. We bring the shopping and our luggage on board and then make ourselves comfortable under the canopy on the aft deck. Fortunately, this will only have to protect us from one thing during the next week – too much sun.

The Peene stretches for almost 100 kilometres through the ice-age moraine landscape of Western Pomerania, unregulated and unspoilt – a small paradise for all those who seek peace and quiet in nature. And this includes not only beavers, otters and sea eagles, but also water enthusiasts in canoes and kayaks, in adventure rafts – or even charter yachts.

Early in the morning we cast off and follow the narrow, dead-straight Neukalen Peenekanal with the sun in our faces for 2 kilometres to Kummerower See, a glittering expanse of water no less than 10 kilometres long and more than 3 kilometres wide. In front of its shallow western shore, just north of the canal, we drop anchor to a depth of 3 metres for a coffee break.

Engine off, silence! Only a warm breeze sweeps over the water. No challenge for the large, silvery iridescent dragonfly, which watches us in hovering flight. The dry reeds crackle and rustle, but nothing can be seen. I wonder which water dweller has its living room in the gloom? In any case, we don't want to disturb them for too long. Anchor up!

Now we follow the Kummerower See to the north-west. Near the small village of Verchen, the Peene – now a proper river – flows out of the lake. At the resting place for waterside walkers on the right bank, there is a relaxed weekend atmosphere. Keep your eyes peeled, because not only a small passenger ferry crosses here, but also the odd swimmer. On the opposite bank is the Aalbude, a destination restaurant that has justifiably achieved a certain regional fame. Here, too, there are moorings along the shore, one of which we take. Fresh fish at a good price!

The middle course of the Peene, which now follows and reaches as far as Demmin at kilometre 30, shows why the designation 'Amazon of the North' is more than just a clever tourist marketing label: the still quite narrow river makes loop after loop, and the few culverts and straight stretches appear just as pristine thanks to the lush nature that pushes into the water.

Wet meadows, spring bogs and floodplains line the banks, oxbow lakes full of reeds pass by, with clumps of birch and alder trees in between. Pines have taken root on sandy elevations, sometimes even mixed and deciduous forest. The most obvious traces of human intervention are the peat excavations on either side, but these nooks and crannies, once cut into the boggy soil during the extraction of the cheap fuel, have long since become lagoons that serve as another refuge for plants and animals. Finally, in 2011, the Flusslandschaft Peene Valley Nature Park was founded, which encompasses the entire river basin.

The scorching sun contributes to the fact that we really feel like we are in the tropics.

A dinghy or canoe is a good way to explore the shallow peat bogs away from the fairway.

The seaside of Usedom is easy to reach (preferably by bike), only a few kilometres from Zinnowitz on the protected Achterwasser. This is a quick way to get to resorts like Koserow, which is less sophisticated but more relaxed, or directly to the Zinnowitz sea bridge, with its villa architecture.

In our imagination, free-standing roots quickly turn into mangroves and grey herons into flamingos. Fortunately, there are no piranhas in the sleepily murmuring stern water, but at most harmless lampreys…

In the middle of the jungle, a towering brick warehouse suddenly appears: Demmin! Shortly before the bascule bridge, we turn left at kilometre 29.5 into an oxbow lake. We

want to get to the water recreation area run by the Blau-Weiß sailing club. The quiet facility with box berths (electricity and water at the pier, bread service) includes a small sanitary building; it is about a kilometre from the town centre. On the way there, before the bascule bridge, you pass the 'Hanseviertel Demmin', enclosed by a wooden palisade. This is a medieval place in summer: you can get an insight into the way of life and crafts from the time when this was a Hanseatic town.

We continue to the city wall, past the colourful houses in the residential area to the very tidy market with the Prussian town hall, reconstructed only a few years ago, and the really imposing tower of St Bartholomaei behind it, a fine example of North German Brick Gothic. In its shadow, so to speak, we

Mooring in the approaches to the shallow and non-navigable peat bogs requires precise local knowledge.

soon stop at the Taverna Alexandros on the market – recommended to us as the best restaurant in Demmin. We liked it too!

Shortly before nine o'clock the following day, we are ready in the headwater of the Kahlden Bridge in Demmin. Like the other two bascule bridges, in Loitz and Anklam, it is too low for larger cabin boats when closed. So there are only three real obstacles to cruising on the whole stretch, but because of the infrequent opening times and the great distances, they require more precise planning than on many an area dominated by locks. The barriers close promptly and the road lifts with

the balance beams, clearing the way for us.

The lower reaches of the Peene begin in Demmin. Two tributaries join it in quick succession: the Tollense at kilometre 29.1 and the Trebel at kilometre 31.2, causing the Peene to double in width and widen its loops. The barely perceptible gradient of only 24 centimetres per 100 kilometres means that the river sometimes flows uphill when there is a persistent east wind.

We occasionally spot homesteads on the more distant heights, and Loitz is the next village we come to right on the shore, here too with a church tower, harbour warehouse and bascule bridge. It was only in 2012 that the modern building at kilometre 42.8 replaced its dilapidated predecessor, which has since been demolished. The village also offers a good marina and moorings along the riverbank in front of the reservoir. Electricity is available everywhere.

The much better option for another stopover in this respect is the Stolpe waterway rest area at kilometre 79.4, where we will spend the night on the way back: the small harbour area at the floating jetty with outriggers is just as good and only a few metres from the terrace of the Stolper Fährkrug, which has been serving travellers for more than 350 years and offers a wide range of specialities on its menu.

It's late afternoon before two more towers rise above the flat landscape downstream. This time it is the Nikolai and Marienkirche churches of Anklam. Perhaps it was the swallows, hawks and crows circling the two towers at lofty heights that inspired Otto Lilienthal, the town's most famous son, to make his daring attempts. The aviation pioneer was born in Anklam in 1848. Today, he is remembered not only by two monuments and a plaque in the town, but also by the Otto Lilienthal Museum, which is well worth seeing, with replicas of his gliders and many models. Visitors on their own boat can moor either (as we did) in the countryside at the waterway rest area at kilometre 87.7 (floating pontoons and pile moorings, water

Neukalen is connected to Lake Kummerow via the narrow Peene Canal.

The narrow Moderortrinne forms the southern part of the Peenestrom.

The harbour of Rankwitz in Lieper Winkel is ideal for excursions, but you can also enjoy the beautiful surroundings on board or in one of the restaurants until the sun sets over the Peene River.

and electricity, waste disposal, sanitary facilities) or directly in the town at the jetty of the boatyard at kilometre 88.9. Our restaurant tip for the evening is the cosy Gaststätte Am Steintor.

After the nightly fog over the river has dissipated under the first strong rays of sunshine, the last leg to the Baltic Sea is on the agenda: at 9:40am the railway bridge opens for us at kilometre 89.1, and shortly afterwards the town and harbour of Anklam lie astern.

After another hour, a rusty disused beacon finally announces the nearby Peene River. Then, without much ceremony, the reed-lined banks recede, and the view opens up to wide waters and the coast of Usedom, about half a nautical mile away to the east. At kilometre 98, we have officially left the Peene; two pairs of barrels bring us to the water, and our bow, under which the brackish water of the Peene River now foams white, swings north-east towards the Zecherin Bridge, whose blue steel structure connects the mainland and the island. With a clear height of 5 metres, it is no obstacle for us even when closed, so that we can approach our first destination on Usedom without delay via the narrow, buoyed Moderort channel.

A white-tailed eagle is on the lookout for prey in a tree near Anklam.

Most harbours in the area indicate guest berths with this yellow wave.

A charter yacht at the jetty in front of the bascule bridge in Loitz.

Neukalen.

The port of Rankwitz is located in the very south of the Lieper Winkel, a peninsula between the Peenestrom and the Achterwasser. The moorings, consisting of pile mooring, box berths and a small swimming facility, are manageable, but here, too, slowing down is a must.

Active people can cycle from here to the Mellenthin moated castle with its famous castle bakery 7 kilometres away, while everyone else can take their own boat to the beach. A good restaurant serving excellent fish indoors and outdoors is the Alte Fischräucherei (Old Fish Smokehouse). The sunset is served for dessert.

We continue north-west until we leave the Peene River at a right angle to Lassan and enter the Achterwasser, the large shallow bay on the inland side of Usedom, between the cardinal buoys Hohe Schar Süd and Warther Haken West with their flanking nets. Here we now also feel the wind from the open Baltic Sea, whose short choppy waves make our *Lotte* buck a little for the first time on this trip.

Our course leads us past the island of Görmitz into the northern part of the Achterwasser until the harbour of Zinnowitz comes into view at its end. Here it is so sheltered again that we can go alongside without swell behind a Grand Banks. But the harbourmaster will not be back until late afternoon. So, what are we waiting for? There is still time in the evening for the pier and the seaside resort architecture of Zinnowitz. Now it's off to Koserow, and the beach.

Text: Christian Tiedt

18 RÜGEN

Lohme in the northeast of Rügen is a
tranquil place with a pretty marina. From
here, Cape Arkona is already in sight.

Circumnavigating Rügen requires careful planning, but it's worth it for the impressive chalk landscape, and the old Hanseatic city, Stralsund.

In five stages, we circumnavigated Germany's largest island – and took a look at the most beautiful harbours.

After starting in the Rhine-Main area, we approached our destination accompanied by a heavy thunderstorm. Even in high summer, weather problems are to be expected on the Baltic Sea. When sailing around Rügen with a motor yacht, careful weather observation and cruise planning are therefore essential.

As we arrive at the Kröslin marina, the rain subsides. There is not much more to do than load the luggage on to our Beneteau Swift Trawler 34 from Yachtcharter Schulz and have dinner in the marina's restaurant. The weather looks good for the next two days. Perfect to start the circumnavigation of the island along the open and more weather-critical eastern and northern flanks. Once into the waters between Rügen and Hiddensee, we can look

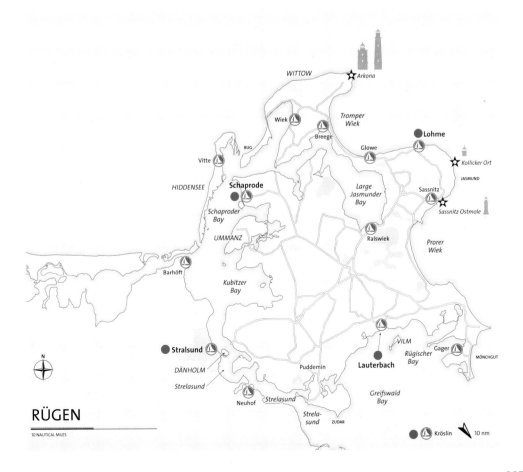

The chalk cliffs on the east coast form an impressive backdrop as you round Rügen.

forward to the rest of the cruise being more relaxing.

At our start the next morning, sun and clouds alternate. It is supposed to remain calm the following day as well. Then comes the next front. So we decide to sail to Lohme for the first night, and the next day we'll sail around the cape to the safe harbour of Schaprode to wait for the front to pass. Those with more stable weather can sail to Sassnitz first and then plan stops in Lohme or Glowe before rounding Cape Arkona.

After leaving Kröslin, we set off buoyed and at reduced speed. A fast trip with the trawler is hardly worth it, because then the Frenchie with her Cummins QSB 5.9 and 425 horsepower becomes a guzzler. When cruising at a comfortable 1,500 revs at a good 7 knots,

we calculate an average consumption of 9.7 litres per hour. So the trawler runs perfectly through the waves. A good five hours pass before the 37 nautical miles to Lohme are completed. On the way, the island's landmark, the famous chalk cliffs, can be seen. The coastal strip is part of the Jasmund National Park, a UNESCO World Heritage Site. The protected area consists of natural beech forests. The spectacle ends at the 117-metre-high Königsstuhl, a particularly prominent cliff a good 2 nautical miles from Lohme. At the next cape we change course to the west and the harbour is already in sight. We go to the jetty right at the entrance, because our lines are too short for the very long box berths. The tour of the town takes us past the well-known Café Niedlich with its magnificent view of

Cape Arkona. In the centre of the village, we come across the restaurant Daheim, clearly the meeting place for visitors. The solid home cooking tastes good and comes at the right time.

Back at the marina, sunset is just around the corner. The perfect time for a walk along the stony coast to a striking boulder with a special history. According to legend, it harbours the island's unborn children, who are brought by the stork or swan, which is why it is called Schwanenstein. There is also a sad story. In the winter of 1956, three boys were playing on the edge of the frozen sea. The ice broke in a storm and they climbed on to the granite boulder for safety, but because of the adverse weather conditions, they could not be rescued in time.

The wind picks up the next day. The sun still shines through occasionally, but the front is approaching. We set off for Cape Arkona. Soon we reach the tip with its striking towers. The smaller lighthouse – a work by the master builder Karl Friedrich Schinkel and the second oldest lighthouse on the German Baltic coast – has long been out of use. The new tower took over navigation duties in 1905. The navy's radio direction finder, put into service in 1927, was destroyed in 1945 and rebuilt in the 1990s. This coastline is also framed by chalk cliffs.

The swell and wind increase at first on our westerly course. Only after we are further into

Stralsund is the gateway to Rügen and its beautiful old town is a particular highlight.

The beautiful harbour of Lohme is a stepping stone to
Bornholm. In high summer, guest berths are often scarce.
Without very long lines it is difficult to moor here.

St John's Church in Schaprode dates from the 13th century and used to help sailors navigate.

There is a water taxi to Hiddensee in the town.

the land cover of Hiddensee does it become calmer. Soon we weave our way into the narrow buoyed fairways and then turn west. If you have more time, you can set course east here and make your way to Ralswiek, one of the oldest settlements on Rügen.

Our destination remains Schaprode. It doesn't take long and we are stuck in a queue. It is Sunday and there is a lot going on. Together with several sailing yachts that are running against the wind under engine power, we have to wait patiently behind a dinghy that is heading towards Hiddensee and crossing in the narrow channel. At the next junction to the south we have free passage again and soon reach the floating jetties in the sheltered natural harbour of Schaprode. The island of Öhe off the harbour to the west offers the best protection from wind and waves. The old fishing village is a popular destination because the ferries to Hiddensee start here. Some fishermen are still active. If you are lucky, you can buy fresh fish directly from the cutter.

The most striking building is the 13th-century St John's Church. The tower used to serve as a navigational aid for seafarers. Many old thatched cottages, often former residences of the captains who used to live here, adorn the village. Schillings Gasthof right at the harbour and the Alte Schule restaurant in the centre of the village offer culinary delights.

According to legend, the Swan Stone in Lohme houses the unborn children of the island.

The bathhouse near Lauterbach is now a spa hotel.

The breeze picks up considerably overnight. As feared, sailing under these conditions is out of the question. We do not regret staying, especially after the reports of our new jetty neighbour, who arrives in the evening. The Dutchman had started in Sweden with his extremely seaworthy two-master and did not have a pleasant crossing with strong winds of up to force 7.

The next morning the sun was shining again. Time to set sail for Stralsund. The 15 nautical miles are covered in two hours. The old Hanseatic city is without doubt one of the highlights of the cruise. The varied and colourful offer starts right in the harbour.

Here, the former sail training ship *Gorch Fock I* awaits visitors. Only a few minutes' walk away is the Ozeaneum with its maritime information. Next is the medieval old town with its remarkable Brick Gothic architecture, which has been protected as a UNESCO World Heritage Site since 2002. The city's important

history becomes clear from the impressive facades of the lovingly restored houses. To get the best perspective of the city, it is worth climbing the tower of St Mary's Church. Here you can get an overview of the historic city centre and the harbour, but the beautiful backdrop also includes Rügen and the bridges that connect the city with the island. It quickly becomes clear from this view why Stralsund is called the 'Gateway to Rügen'.

After the descent, you can visit the German Maritime Museum, which is only a few minutes away, or reward yourself with a refreshing drink in one of the many pubs in the old town. The city also offers a wide range of evening activities.

When you continue your journey the next day, you first pass the bridge to Rügen. With the Swift Trawler 34's equipment carrier in place, there is no need to observe opening times, the height is fine. Our last destination is Lauterbach. With the town harbour and the

Lauterbach marina, there are two adjacent harbours to choose from, but they are managed together. We find a lovely berth at the jetty in the town harbour. The pretty view has its disadvantages, however, because the sanitary facilities are in the marina and necessitate a short walk. This leads directly past the railway station, which lies between the two parts of the harbour. From here, the famous seaside resorts of Binz and Sellin on the east coast, with their stretches of white sandy beaches and impressive piers, can be reached by the historic narrow-gauge railway, also known as the 'Racing Roland'.

You should plan a whole day to swim at the beautiful beaches and to explore the culinary offerings. In the evening, you can return to Lauterbach in comfort on the old steam train. We can also recommend a pleasant walk. It leads into the Goor forest area near Lauterbach, part of the Goor-Muglitz nature reserve. The bathhouse, with its imposing columned hall, was built by Prince Wilhelm Malte I of Putbus in 1818 and today serves as a spa hotel. Nature lovers will appreciate the hiking trail through the park. The next day we have to be back in Kröslin. The 20 nautical miles are completed in less than three hours. After a wonderful week of sailing with many wonderful experiences and insights, we start our long return journey the same day.

Text: Dieter Wanke

Waiting for visitors in Stralsund harbour.

19 BORNHOLM

Between Hygge and Legerwall – pointers for sailing around Bornholm from a local in his Najad 34.

'You want to go to Bornholm?' asks the girlfriend, thinking for a moment. And then she says, 'No problem.' There is one obstacle for sailors: you can't charter on this small Danish outpost. The only way to get there is on your own boat. And that takes time. From Sassnitz on Rügen alone it is 50 nautical miles, heading north-east – a good day's journey to the island with its heart of granite and its harbours blasted into the rocks. With a lot of wind, it can be quite a sporting affair. But I have the good fortune to be in a relationship with a Danish woman, and her home is a big village. Within a radius of a few kilometres, everyone knows everyone else. A sailor, too, of course. In addition, family and 'hygge'

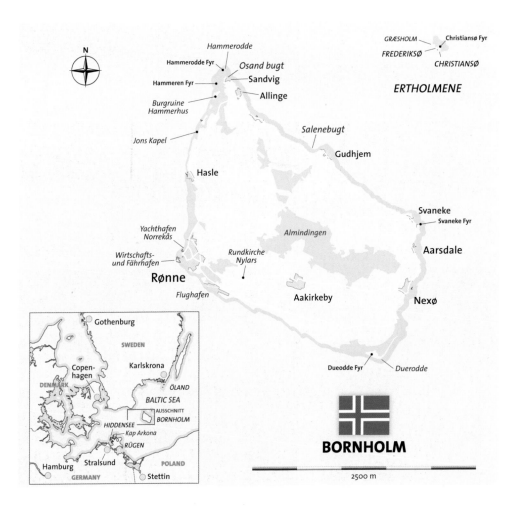

This is where smoked fish is produced.

Smoked fish for sale in the Hasle Røgeri on the west coast.

Gudhjem Marina is one of Bornholm's most popular places to moor.

are very important there. Hygge stands for cosiness and enjoying life. The Danes are pros at this: for years they have been number one in the 'World Happiness Report'.

My friend calls her cousin – and she already has a contact: our maritime man is called Rune Holm, and he seems to be made for showing us Bornholm from the point of view of a yachtsman who knows his way around. The only answer to a long email to him was: 'When are you coming?'

Rune is employed by the Bornholm Business Centre. Officially, he is a 'consultant for newcomers'; he helps them to settle on the island. Bornholm is happy about every newcomer at the moment. Unofficially, Rune is a Danish jack of all trades. He seems to

know every one of the 40,000 islanders and every spot on the 60,000-hectare island. But what's even better: Rune has a boat and wants to go sailing with us.

Two weeks later we meet him at probably the most beautiful place on the island, a kiosk called 'Syd-Øst for Paradis', 'South-East of Paradise', right by the lighthouse in Svaneke – one of the most charming places on Bornholm. Rune sits on a chair overlooking the small beach with its diving tower. A band plays live music. It's really hyggelig here! Rune nods. He himself moved to the island, which has the most hours of sunshine in the country, only a few years ago. Tomorrow too? He pulls out his smartphone and frowns: it's supposed to be windy. Rune suggests a quick nip to the east coast.

Once you have made it through the harbour entrance to Christiansø, you are rewarded with an idyll.

Nowhere in Denmark does the sun shine more often than on Bornholm, including here in Sveke's harbour.

The next morning, shortly before six o'clock, there is a fresh breeze in Svaneke harbour. But it smells of coffee when we enter Rune's boat. It's an old Najad 34 – the very first model from Olle Enderlein's shipyard. Rune tells us that he has never got wet in his spacious cockpit with its large sprayhood. That is about to change…

But first, the diesel engine warms up in neutral. Rune hands out life jackets and unties the lines. Apart from us, only the baker in Svaneke is up at this time of day. The girlfriend knows this because it is her cousin, who bakes sourdough bread. To starboard, the lighthouse glows in the first sunlight of the day. To port, the first signs of smoke appear – they come from the chimneys of a local smokehouse.

If anything is typical of Bornholm, it is smoked fish! Rune says somewhat wistfully that the fish has long since had to be bought from the North Sea, the local fish is no longer sufficient. Apart from that, he raves about his adopted home: 'Bornholm is booming! The island has potential and is becoming more and more popular.' Not only for holidays, but also for living. In the next few years, a lot of jobs will become available. In demand are doctors, architects, craftsmen, bakers…

'We need almost everyone,' says Rune, adding, 'Nobody needs to be afraid of island fever here either.'

It is good to stop here for a while – not only at the harbour wall of Svaneke, but on Bornholm in general.

Bornholm has an airport, and there are flights to Copenhagen several times a day. But why go far away at all? For sailors, the island is a dream: no place is further than 10 kilometres from the water. It never takes more than a quarter of an hour from the idea of setting sail after work to setting sail.

We sail up the east coast downwind. 'How about breakfast in Gudhjem and back around noon?' asks Rune. 'And tomorrow to Christiansø?' The latter is part of the pea islands, the outpost of the outpost to the north-east. Small rocky islands and a magically attractive gem. We nod, all right. Or almost. We are barely half a mile out when the heavy long keel begins to buck against the short, steep Baltic wave.

With my not-so-seaworthy girlfriend in mind, I ask for an alternative. Perhaps a round sail to Nexø in the south? Rune shakes his head. 'Not attractive,' he says. Or to a nice anchorage somewhere? To the white beach at Dueodde

on the southern tip? 'A bit far,' says Rune, 'and rarely quiet enough.' In other words, he only has his anchor for decoration. There is nothing on the west coast with these conditions either, he says. That's why most of the cosy harbours are on the east coast. After all, there are no fewer than 11 of them. We decide to turn around and head down the coast a bit, past the lighthouse. It's only a small manoeuvre, but it's like the difference between day and night: the position of the sun is the same, but its intensity is twice as strong. At these temperatures, even the girlfriend's facial expressions thaw. What follows is very relaxed first-class in front of a beautiful archipelago landscape.

The next day the wind picks up a little more. Too much, Rune thinks. There is no sail to be seen on the water, only whitecaps. It's the perfect time for some land-based research: we take a rental car and drive to the rugged west coast to look at some of the few harbours upwind. And of course Hammershus – the largest castle ruin in the northern hemisphere, perched on a cliff above the sea. From up there you have a fantastic view. And the full force of the wind. The waves crash against the coast at almost one-second intervals.

Hammerhavn lies at the foot of the 13th-century ruins. In the past, granite was shipped from here, among other things for the construction of the Kiel Canal. Today, visiting sailors can look down on the ruins from the cockpit of their yacht – and can theoretically chug into the surrounding grottos in their dinghy or excursion boat. But not now, with onshore gusts of up to force 7.

We drive down the west coast towards Rønne, the island's capital. A string of charming harbours follows: Vang, Teglkås, Helligpeder. For sailors, they are best described as small, smaller, smallest. They are easily accessible in a Nordic Folkboat. Skippers of larger yachts, however, need more courage to navigate them – and perhaps a bow thruster. But once you've made it, it's an idyllic place to lie.

In Hasle we stop at the Hasle Røgeri. Time to taste some smoked fish. Connoisseurs eat 'Sol over Gudhjem' – 'Sun over Gudhjem': this is smoked herring with red onions, radishes, chopped chives, pepper and grainy sea salt on brown bread. A raw egg yolk is poured over the dish to represent the sun. A tasty consolation on days like these.

The next morning, we sail anyway. We venture on the 'great passage' to the small pea islands – across to Christiansø. The horizon at Svaneke looks deceptively calm, but the wind is still blowing hard. The second half of our ride becomes rough: an upwind course with unpleasant 2-metre Baltic waves, no matter how

If you moor in Hammerhavn in the north of the island, you have a view of the old fortress ruins of Hammershus.

smoothly a long keeler sets into the water. The girlfriend asks pointedly, 'How much longer?'

Unfortunately, we don't quite make the height on arrival and have to tack again south of the harbour entrance at the offshore seal rock. Why don't we just take the entrance to leeward – that is, behind the island? 'There are no moorings there,' says Rune.

The harbour entrance of Christiansø is located upwind and can seem quite daunting. It's quite narrow, with shoaling on the port side in front of the jetty. The surf breaks on the coast only a boat's length away. The spirit is willing, even if the stomach is weak. But we are practically on the finish line.

A minute later, boat and sense of balance

A rainbow over the charming marina of Svaneke on the east coast.

The view of the sea tempts us to stay, but we have to leave again. Our rodeo ride begins at the harbour exit. There it happens, a first: Rune has to duck away from the waves! After 11 nautical miles we arrive back in Svaneke – and feel like we've crossed the Bay of Biscay. Rocked about, but happy.

On the last day, Rune sails with us along the pearls of the east coast: Gudhjem, Allinge and Sandvig. With a stopover in Listed, or to be more precise, at Ib Hansen – harbourmaster of passion. 'German sailors in particular love the personal service I offer,' says Ib, who still collects the money himself, assigns berths and helps with mooring.

And why are so many of his berths empty? 'The fees were increased in 2015. A mistake – the sailors stayed away. So the prices were lowered again,' says Ib Hansen. 'But word hasn't got around yet.' Those who moor with an elegant classic or perfect harbour manoeuvre at his place in Listed are sometimes allowed to moor for a night for free, he says. Bornholm is far too beautiful not to be visited at least once a year.

Rune nods. If it were up to him, we could stay right there. He would help with the immigration. It would be tempting! A life in the middle of the Baltic Sea – nowhere further than 10 kilometres from the sea.

Text: Jan Jepsen

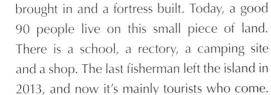

are calm again in the water off Christiansø – which was originally a pure rock island. But in the 17th century, King Christian V had earth brought in and a fortress built. Today, a good 90 people live on this small piece of land. There is a school, a rectory, a camping site and a shop. The last fisherman left the island in 2013, and now it's mainly tourists who come.

LIST OF CONTRIBUTORS

Michael Amme is a photographer and author from Hamburg. He regularly travels for the *Yacht* in various areas. www.michaelamme.de

Marc Bielefeld lives in Hamburg as a freelance journalist and author for various magazines and daily newspapers, including the *Yacht*. www.lets-sea.com

Andreas Fritsch is an editor at *Yacht*, where he heads the travel department.

Lisa Harms grew up in the Opti and dared to take the big plunge with her new H-dinghy with her boyfriend, Sebastian Völkel, during a university semester break.

Jan Jepsen is a journalist and author from Hamburg and travels around the world for various magazines, including *Yacht*.

Sönke Roever sailed around the world from 2007 to 2010, works as a freelancer and photographer for the *Yacht* and is the author of several sailing books. He also offers Blau Wasser seminars with his wife, Judith. www.blauwasser.de

Hauke Schmidt is an editor at *Yacht*, where he is primarily responsible for testing and technology.

Morten Strauch is a photographer and has been travelling for *Yacht* and *boote* for years. Now he has joined Hanse Yachts in Greifswald. www.mortenstrauch.de

Christian Tiedt is an editor at *boote* and travels for the travel section in various regions, on rivers, lakes and seas.

Dieter Wanke is a photographer, not only on but also under water. www.dieterwanke.de

INDEX